New Beginnings

New Beginnings

WRITING WITH FLUENCY

Diane Fitton
Monroe Community College

Barbara Warner
Monroe Community College

HOUGHTON MIFFLIN COMPANY   Boston   New York

Senior Sponsoring Editor: Mary Jo Southern
Associate Editor: Kellie Cardone
Editorial Assistant: Danielle Richardson
Associate Project Editor: Sarah Godshall
Manufacturing Manager: Florence Cadran
Senior Marketing Manager: Nancy Lyman

Cover design: Dutton & Sherman Design
Cover image: ©David La Fleur/SIS

CREDITS

Page 3: Robert B. Jackson, *Road Race Round the World: New York to Paris, 1908.* Copyright © 1977. Reprinted by permission of the author.

Page 42: Marty Meitus, Rocky Mountain News Food Editor. Originally published in the Rocky Mountain News, August 23, 1995. Reprinted with permission of the Denver Rocky Mountain News.

Page 72: Reprinted by permission of the author.

Page 100: Dianne J. Moore, a social worker and freelance writer, lives in Phoenix, Arizona, where she moved due to the harsh winters of Michigan. She conducts seminars nationwide and is a member of the American Society of Journalists and Authors.

Page 128: Pam Easton, "Texas Man, Georgia Friend Pushing for Civility," from the Associated Press, March 21, 1999. Reprinted by permission.

Page 210: Reprinted from the Introduction to BEST-LOVED FOLKTALES OF THE WORLD, edited by Joanna Cole by special permission of Guild America® Books, an imprint of Doubleday Direct, Inc. © 1982 by Joanna Cole.

Page 240: This document can be found at: www.nidlink.com/~bobhard/seattle.html

Page 266: David Mahoney and Richard Restak, M.D., *The Longevity Strategy: How to Live to 100 Using the Brain-Body Connection,* Copyright © 1998. Reprinted by permission of John Wiley & Sons, Inc.

Printed in the U.S.A.

Library of Congress Catalog Card Number: 00-104444

ISBN: 0-618-00494-7

123456789-DOC-04 03 02 01 00

CONTENTS

v

PREFACE

What started several years ago as a casual conversation about teaching developmental English ended up with our realizing that we, the authors, had similar pedagogical approaches. Given our combined forty years of experience and, what we considered a compelling methodology, we set ourselves the challenge of creating an "ideal" developmental English textbook.

New Beginnings is based on two assumptions about its audience. The first is that most adult learners enrolled in a developmental English course need to improve their reading proficiency and build academic knowledge. Materials included in the textbook, therefore, provide exposure to reading that both interests the students and allows them to develop the basic reading skills they need for academic work. In addition, the material fosters an awareness of academic knowledge that students can build on. *New Beginnings* includes models of good writing, information to advance cultural literacy, and exercises to engender thinking.

A second assumption is that students in developmental English classes need instruction to articulate their thoughts in meaningful written sentences. Traditional grammar instruction, isolated from the task of composing sentences, typically fails to make a measurable difference in the way these students write. The sentence exercises in *New Beginnings* incorporate the linguistic principles of sentence rearrangement and sentence combining resulting in students learning to construct grammatically correct sentences. Designed to be progressively challenging, the sentence exercises encourage students to become increasingly fluent. By applying the sentence skills they have developed, students can, with confidence, write their own paragraphs using personal experience as well as source material.

The task we set for ourselves was ambitious. For more than a year we field-tested readings and activities in English classes. Using various "drafts" of the emerging text, we became encouraged by our observations. Our weakest students made solid, steady progress, while at the same time, students who were simply filling "gaps" in their reading and writing skills excelled. The text worked for our morning, afternoon, and evening classes, adapting to sections that met two or three times a week. More important, our students verbalized how much they enjoyed the work. What we recognized was that students using *New Beginnings* were becoming capable students of the English language as well as enthusiastic lifelong learners.

New Beginnings offers the following features:

Reading Comprehension Skills

Each chapter focuses on a topic designed to promote cultural literacy and reading comprehension. High-interest reading selections challenge adult learners to learn information, explore ideas, and evaluate content. Where indicated, vocabulary definitions are included to facilitate fluent reading.

Sentence Development

Sentence rearrangement and combining activities progress sequentially within each chapter for skill development. These exercises start with *structured* exercises from which students learn patterns other than the typical subject-verb beginnings. The final exercises, *unstructured* or open sentence combining, promote flexibility in sentence construction and motivate students to consider sentence meaning and emphasis.

Grammar in Context

Sentence-rearrangement and sentence-combining activities teach the principles of grammar in a meaningful way. Students learn how to change the grammatical form of a sentence (the surface structure) while retaining the sentence syntax (the deep structure). A final chapter, a concise reference for grammar and mechanics, uses thought-provoking quotations to model each point of grammar or mechanics and includes exercises to check understanding.

Writing from Experience

Students respond on a personal level to one of a variety of thematically related writing topics. The first four choices include prewriting prompts. After writing a draft of the paragraph, students revise by applying the sentence-rearrangement and sentence-combining skills they have practiced in the chapter. In the editing stage, students use a checklist of important criteria.

Writing from Resources

Students practice expository writing by locating and paraphrasing information in response to questions related to the chapter's topic. They develop skills using the library and Internet.

Activities-Based Skills

The questions and exercises throughout the textbook lend themselves easily to a variety of methodologies including whole group, individual, partner, and collaborative learning. It has been the authors' experience that exercises should not dictate the method of learning, but rather the dynamics of the group and the needs of the students should determine the appropriate learning process.

Recursive Learning

One striking advantage of *New Beginnings* is its adaptability to diverse student abilities, curriculum needs, and semester formats within a developmental English program. After the first teaching chapter, the remaining nine chapters are sequenced independently to provide recursive learning of writing and reading skills. This feature provides the instructor autonomy in deciding how to maximize use of the text.

Acknowledgments

We would like to acknowledge the numerous students from our classes at Monroe Community College who reinforced our efforts as we developed *New Beginnings.* In addition, we offer our appreciation to Judi Salsburg, Ellen Baker, and Matthew Fox in the Transitional Studies Department at Monroe Community College for offering their suggestions to the Instructor's Manual.

Second, we thank the many reviewers who offered suggestions:

William Abernathy, Washtenaw Community College
Marlys Cordoba, College of the Siskiyous
Judy D. Covington, Trident Technical College
Phyllis Boatman, Southern Arkansas University Tech
Larry Carlson, Orange Coast College
Jennifer Hurd, Harding University
Tamara Kuzmenkov, Tacoma Community College
Karen H. Soutar, Aims Community College
Linda J. Whisnant, Guilford Technical Community College
Paul Wolford, Walters State Community College

Third, our sincere gratitude is extended to the staff at Houghton Mifflin Company, including Mary Jo Southern, Jennifer Roderick, Kellie Cardone, Sarah Godshall, and Liz Napolitano, who helped bring this textbook to fruition, and to Suzanne Hinderliter, with whom we first discussed writing a textbook for our students.

Finally, special tribute must go to our respective families for their helpful suggestions and unwavering support and encouragement. To John, who unselfishly and tirelessly helped us unravel the complexities of our computers and software and cooked us many dinners so we could devote more time to writing our textbooks, we give our heartfelt thanks.

Diane Fitton
Barbara Warner

New
Beginnings

CHAPTER 1

Auto Racing

*Patience, persistence and perspiration make an
unbeatable combination for success.*

— Napolean Hill

It may be hard to imagine that auto racing and writing have anything in common, but perhaps they do. Before a race, the racer who wants to perform well spends days studying the racetrack. In much the same way, before writing a paper, a writer who wants to write well thinks about the topic. After the racer considers the track, he or she goes out on practice runs. Similarly, while thinking about the topic, a writer writes many drafts. The racer finally commits his or her talents on the day of the race; likewise, a writer produces a final draft for the day the paper is due. Both racing and writing involve knowing what is to be done, setting up a schedule for the work, and then accomplishing the task.

Success comes from using experience as well as new information as a base for increasing skills. The writing experience you have had gives you background to build on. *New Beginnings* provides you with what may be new information about writing sentences and paragraphs. Each chapter starts with a reading on a topic of general interest. As you read, you can gather information about the topic and learn more about writing by observing how a professional writer has expressed ideas.

Race car driving combines speed, technology, and mental agility. The reading in this chapter is about one of the world's earliest automobile races.

Connecting Reading with Writing

EXERCISE 1   Reflections on Auto Racing

1. What do you think are the physical and psychological skills involved in driving a race car?

   _____

   _____

   _____

2. Why is it that winning a race often depends on both the car and the driver?

   _____

   _____

   _____

Road Race Round the World—
New York to Paris, 1908

by Robert B. Jackson

1   On a cold Lincoln's Birthday morning, in 1908, six automobiles lined up in front of a cheering crowd in Times Square, New York City. They were about to start the longest and most difficult road race ever to be held—from New York to Paris.

2   The route of their rugged contest had been planned to take them across the United States to the West Coast, then north into Canada and Alaska. Crossing the ice of the frozen Bering Strait, they would next race across the vast expanses of Siberia and Russia. After speeding through Europe, they were to finish their amazing seventeen-thousand-mile race in Paris.

3   The New York to Paris race is all the more remarkable because it took place during the very early days of the automobile. The race was held hardly sixteen years after the two Duryea brothers built the first successful gasoline automobile in the United States. In 1896, automobiles were so rare that one was exhibited in the Barnum and Bailey Circus; but in 1908, only a dozen years later, courageous motorists were preparing to race their frail cars nearly around the world.

4   Most automobile experts of the time predicted that the cars would not be able to finish the race. The automobiles of 1908 were underpowered and uncomfortable. More important, they were not reliable. They broke down frequently and often they would not even start. Many reporters, who had seen motorists labor half a day to get their cars running and then make several repair stops during a twenty-mile trip, thought that the entrants were foolhardy to attempt a seventeen-thousand-mile trip.

5   Such a race was thought to be impossible for other reasons as well. Roads were scarce and poorly made in those days. Not many gas stations or garages were in existence as yet. The event was to start in the dead of winter, crossing the difficult open country and jagged mountains of three continents—ice, snow, swamps and mud would be certain to slow and stop the cars. Also, few people lived along much of the lengthy route, and widely separated telegraph stations were the only means of fast communication in most places.

6   But there was a small group of men who had great confidence in the cars they manufactured, owned or drove. They believed that the automobile had an important future, and they wanted to prove that cars could be depended upon to cover long distances quickly. What better way of calling attention to the reliability of automobiles than a dangerous and demanding long-distance competition?

7   On February 12, six confident teams, anxious to begin the demanding test, drove their cars to the starting line at 43rd Street and Seventh Avenue. The short entry list was an international one. There were three French cars and one Italian car, one German and one from the United States. They were not special racing cars but regular road automobiles of the time, with large wooden-spoked wheels, bicycle-type fenders and big brass headlights. However, each car had been specially prepared and equipped for the strenuous race ahead.

8   As the competitors assembled on the starting line, brass bands blared their national anthems and sprawling crowds of 250,000 New Yorkers pushed closer to catch a glimpse of the cars and their strikingly dressed crews. Some of the teams had prepared for the piercing cold ahead by wearing shaggy bearskin coats and large fur hats. Others, with less foresight, sported yachting caps and kid gloves. A few poorly informed motorists even wore patent-leather shoes and spats.

9   Shortly before 11 A.M., a trumpet call signaled the drivers to start their engines. At 11:15, the starter climbed to his stand, raised a gold pistol in the air, and fired. The six cars roared forward, the crowd cheered loudly, and the New York to Paris race was under way.

10   Late in the evening of July 30, five and a half months later, great crowds lined the streets of Paris to see the American car, the Thomas, arrive. Although an unimpressed policeman almost gave a ticket to the Americans for driving without headlights, the Parisians eagerly hailed the victors. A French cyclist offered his bicycle light to the Americans as replacement for their broken headlamps; and when it could not be detached, he was pulled aboard, bicycle and all.

11   The American driver, George Schuster, drove the battered Thomas to the offices of *Le Matin,* the sponsoring newspaper, where the race committee officially proclaimed the American entry to be the winner of the New York to Paris race. The Thomas had covered 13,341 miles on its own power and traveled 8,569 additional miles by water, all within 170 days. Counting only the time spent on the road, the Thomas had averaged 152 miles a day, a memorable accomplishment for that era.

12   So ended one of the most astounding chapters of automotive history. Three teams of hardy, resourceful, and courageous motorists had successfully raced automobiles nearly around the globe at a time when most people thought cars were either expensive playthings or newfangled contraptions certain to break down. Both men and cars had survived the rigors of their hard, dangerous journey to earn the admiration and respect of the world.

After you have completed the reading, check your comprehension by answering some questions. Responding to these questions and understanding the correct choices give you skill and confidence in using the multiple choice format common in many college classes. Just as important, your ability to understand what others write gives you insight into how to express your own ideas.

EXERCISE 2   Questions About the Reading

Select the letter that best completes each question or statement.

1. This passage focuses on
    A.   an auto race of 1908.
    B.   automobiles in 1908.
    C.   driving conditions in 1908.
    D.   racing competitions in 1908.

2. Choose the sentence that tells the main idea of the passage.
    A.   Automobile experts thought the road race would be uncomfortable.
    B.   The road race was a daring undertaking.
    C.   The road race would take a very long time.
    D.   Cars were not as good as they are today.

3. Which of the following is not mentioned in this passage as a challenge for the motorists?
    A.   underpowered car engines
    B.   poor roads
    C.   bad maps
    D.   terrible weather

4. We might conclude from this passage that
    A.   the road race publicized the automobile around the world.
    B.   the road race united people around the world.
    C.   all of the cars finished the race.
    D.   none of the cars finished the race.

5. The American team pulled the Parisian bicycle into the Thomas because

    A. the Parisian cyclist was in the way of the American car.

    B. the Parisian cyclist wanted to show a spirit of international cooperation.

    C. the American team wanted to avoid getting a ticket for speeding.

    D. the American team wanted to avoid getting a ticket for driving without headlights.

6. As used in the sentence, "However, each car had been specially prepared and equipped for the strenuous race ahead," the word *strenuous* means

    A. long.

    B. hard.

    C. time-consuming.

    D. physical.

Sentence Explication

In this exercise you learn how to paraphrase and evaluate sentences, a skill that is valuable when you use other people's ideas in your writing. The first part of the exercise involves paraphrasing the sentence, that is, rewriting the sentence using your own words. A dictionary and a thesaurus are useful for this activity. The results of paraphrasing will, of course, vary, but a paraphrased sentence must include all the given ideas and no added ones.

Example

1. Either use the sentence that follows or select and copy a different sentence from the reading selection.

    Not many gas stations or garages were in existence as yet.

                                        paragraph #5

2. Paraphrase the sentence by rewriting it in your own words.

    There were few places to get fuel or to have a car fixed at that time.

3. React to the sentence. What comments and questions do you have about it?

    What did the gas stations look like? What services were offered? What was the cost of gas? Of repairs? In what ways were the racers affected? Where or how did they get fuel when there were no stations?

4.   Relate to the sentence. What personal experiences does it bring to mind?

> *The sentence made me think about what it must have been like to travel in 1908. In some ways, it must have been great to have the sense of space that must have existed in 1908. Then the world was so much less developed than it is now. People didn't have many material things. Of course, they wouldn't have known anything different.*
>
> *The sentence brings to mind a time about midnight when a friend and I were driving on a highway that passed through hundreds of miles of swamplands. We suddenly noticed that the fuel gauge was on empty. We had no idea how far we would have to drive to a gas station. We had not noticed a station or any other vehicle since the highway had started into the swamp. If the car stalled, we would likely be in the swamp for the rest of the night.*

Now try Exercise 3 on your own.

EXERCISE 3   Sentence Explication

1.   Use either the sentence that follows or select and copy a different sentence from the reading selection.

> *Each car had been specially prepared and equipped for the strenuous race ahead.*

paragraph #7

Or the sentence you choose:

_____

_____

paragraph #____

2.   Paraphrase the sentence by rewriting it in your own words.

_____

_____

_____

_____

3. React to the sentence. What comments and questions do you have about it?

_____

_____

_____

_____

_____

4. Relate to the sentence. What personal experiences does it bring to mind?

_____

_____

_____

_____

_____

_____

_____

EXERCISE 4   Questions for Writing and Discussion

1. What happened in the world of automobiles between 1896 and 1908?

2. What were the limitations of automobiles in 1908?

3. Why were the participants enthusiastic about the race? What showed that many of them were naïve?

4. Using the information given in the reading, calculate the Thomas's speed per hour. Explain your reasoning.

Working from Sentences to Paragraph

Rearrange Sentences with New Beginnings

The beginning words of a sentence provide a focus for that sentence. Since the majority of sentences begin with the subject of the sentence, most sentences are focused on **who** or **what** is doing something. The following sentence begins with telling *what* the sentence is about, *the horseless carriage.*

> The **"horseless carriage"** made its debut at Chicago's Columbia Exposition in 1893.

However, you do not need to start every sentence with the subject. Other parts of the sentence can be emphasized by putting them at the beginning. Various arrangements can create different emphases without changing the meaning of the sentence. With an awareness of the power of a sentence's beginning, you can focus on what is most important. An additional benefit of varying sentence beginnings is creating a pleasing pattern that makes sentences read rhythmically.

A sentence can be rearranged to change focus or emphasis by moving parts of the sentence. The focus of a sentence can change from **who** or **what** to **where, when, why,** or **how.** Often, this rearrangement can be accomplished simply by moving words from one location in the sentence to another location.

Since your goal in writing is to arrange words that focus your ideas to convey the meaning you intend, choose the sentence that best expresses your idea.

---

*The road doesn't tell the traveler what
lies ahead.*

— Bantu proverb

NEW BEGINNINGS FOR SENTENCES

who or **what**	**The "horseless carriage"** triumphantly made its debut at Chicago's Exposition in 1893 to demonstrate the potential of the automobile.
where	**At Chicago's Exposition** in 1893, the "horseless carriage" triumphantly made its debut to demonstrate the potential of the automobile.
when	**In 1893,** the "horseless carriage" triumphantly made its debut at Chicago's Exposition to demonstrate the potential of the automobile.
why	**To demonstrate the potential of the automobile,** the "horseless carriage" triumphantly made its debut at Chicago's Exposition in 1893.
how	**Triumphantly,** the "horseless carriage" made its debut at Chicago's Exposition in 1893 to demonstrate the potential of the automobile.

EXERCISE 5   Cow Pastures and Sandy Beaches

Part A

Use the provided new sentence beginnings to change the emphasis of the following sentences that describe how stock car racing began in the United States. As you rearrange the words, be sure to keep the meaning of the original sentence.

1.   During the 1940s, in the southern part of the United States, a favorite pastime for youthful car drivers was to race one another.

   In the southern part of the United States, _____

   EXAMPLE

   In the southern part of the United States during the 1940s, a favorite pastime for youthful car drivers was to race one another.

2. The cars were called "stock cars" because they were basic, stripped-down cars straight off the assembly line.

   Because they were _____

   EXAMPLE

   Because they were basic, stripped down cars straight off the assembly line, these cars were called "stock cars."

3. The drivers laid out a track in a cow pasture and started racing.

   After laying out a track in a cow pasture _____

   _____

   _____

4. The long, smooth beaches in Daytona, Florida became, in time, favorite places for stock car racing.

   In time, favorite places _____

   _____

   _____

5. The race along the sand dunes was watched by thousands of spectators.

   Thousands of spectators _____

   _____

   _____

6. Often the tide came in before the race was completely over.

   Before the race was completely over, _____

   _____

   _____

7. In 1947 the stock car drivers formed a club called the National Association of Stock Car Auto Racing, NASCAR.

The National Association of Stock Car Racing _____

_____

_____

Part B

After checking your rearranged sentences with your instructor, copy them to create a paragraph.

Combine Sentences with New Beginnings

Read the following sentences about the 1908 automobile race.

> Snow had been the largest problem east of Chicago. The big difficulty west of the Windy City was mud. This happened during the day. The mud was sticky ooze. The mud gripped the cars like glue. It made them slide out of control. In some places, the mud was so thick. The cars stalled going *down* steep hills. At night the mud froze. The cars bounced over bone-jarring ruts.

Look at the way author Robert Jackson wrote the sentences:

> Snow had been the largest problem east of Chicago, **but** the big difficulty west of the Windy City was mud. **During the day,** the mud was sticky ooze **that either** gripped the cars like glue **or** made them slide out of control. In some places, the mud was so thick **that** cars stalled going *down* steep hills. At night the mud froze, **and** the cars bounced over bone-jarring ruts.

You will most likely agree that the second paragraph is easier to read because the combined sentences convey more clearly the author's meaning. By combining, or joining, the first two sentences with the word *but,* the author is showing contrast. The combined next four sentences improve fluency. Separated, the sentences are choppy and the ideas lack connection. The last two sentences are combined in order to show that two things happened at the same time—the mud froze *and* the cars bounced.

Now read other sentences about the auto race.

> The Thomas was damaged. It was coated with mud and grime from around the world. It was crated and shipped back to the United States.

Many joyful celebrations were held. The largest reception took place in New York City. The Thomas crew drove their weather-beaten car from City Hall up to Times Square. Times Square was the starting point for their ordeal. Then, Schuster, Miller, and Roberts drove the Thomas out to Sagamore Hill on Long Island. There they met President Theodore Roosevelt. He congratulated them upon their amazing achievement.

Compare the way the author wrote the sentences:

The damaged Thomas, **still** coated with mud and grime from around the world, was crated and shipped back to the United States, **where** many joyful celebrations were held. The largest reception took place in New York City, **when** the Thomas crew drove their weather-beaten car from City Hall up to Times Square, the starting point for their ordeal. Then, Schuster, Miller, and Roberts drove the Thomas out to Sagamore Hill on Long Island to meet President Theodore Roosevelt, **who** congratulated them upon their amazing achievement.

Note especially how ideas from several sentences have been combined or written as one sentence. What effect does the combining have on the meaning?

In the following exercise you practice combining clusters of sentences using an indicated sentence beginning.

---

*Knowledge is power, but enthusiasm pulls
the switch.*

— Ivern Ball

EXERCISE 6   California Hot Wheels

Part A

Read the following draft of a paragraph about drag racing. In Parts B and C, you will work on combining sentences and adding transitions to make the paragraph coherent.

A drag race is a competition between two vehicles. The race begins at a standing start. There are accepted standards for the distance. That distance is a quarter mile. Or that distance is an eighth mile. Drag racing began in California. This happened during the postwar years of the 1940s. The competitions began with two drivers. The two drivers met on a public highway. They raced each other over a stretch of public highway. The cars were built for acceleration. The cars raced in high-speed sprints. Drag races moved to dried-up lakebeds in the desert. The two cars raced a quarter-mile dash. In 1950, drag racing became a ticket event. The event was held on the runways at Orange County Airport in southern California. The National Hot Rod Association (NHRA) was formed soon after. It was formed to establish rules for the new sport.

Part B

Combine the ideas from the sentences in each group to write one new sentence. Begin the new sentence *using the indicated words*. As you write the sentence, think about the emphasis and relationships you want to achieve.

1.

A drag race is a competition between two vehicles.

The race begins at a standing start.

A drag race _____

> EXAMPLE
>
> *A drag race is a competition between two vehicles that begins at a standing start.*

2.

There are accepted standards for the distance.

That distance is a quarter mile.

That distance is an eighth mile.

The accepted standards _____

> EXAMPLE
>
> *The accepted standards for the distance are a quarter mile and an eighth mile.*

3.

Drag racing began in California.

This happened during the postwar years of the 1940s.

During _____

_____

_____

_____

4.

The competitions began with two drivers.

The two drivers met on a public highway.

They raced each other over a stretch of public highway.

The competitions _____

_____

_____

_____

5.

The cars were built for acceleration.

The cars raced in high-speed sprints.

Built for acceleration _____

_____

_____

_____

6.

Drag races moved to dried-up lakebeds in the desert.

The two cars raced a quarter-mile dash.

Drag races _____

_____

_____

_____

7.

In 1950, drag racing became a ticket event.

The event was held on the runways at Orange County Airport in southern California.

In 1950, _____

_____

_____

_____

8.

The National Hot Rod Association (NHRA) was formed soon after.

It was formed to establish rules for the new sport.

Soon after _____

_____

_____

_____

Part C

After checking your combined sentences with your instructor, copy them to create a paragraph. Note the differences between the original and the rewritten paragraphs.

Combine Sentences on Your Own

In the following exercise, you decide how to combine clusters of sentences.

---

*Perseverance is not a long race; it is many
short races one after the other.*

— Walter Elliott

EXERCISE 7   Powered by the Sun

Part A

Read the following draft of an informative paragraph describing an innovative car race. In Parts B and C, you will work on combining sentences and adding transitions to make the paragraph coherent.

The Sun Rayce is an unusual car race. It takes place every two years. It is sponsored by the U.S. Energy Department, General Motors Corporation, and EDS. It lasts ten days. College teams build and drive their own solar race cars. The cars are powered only by electricity from solar panels. To qualify for the race, the team's solar car must be able to travel a minimum of 125 miles. The team's solar car must have a lap speed of at least 25 miles per hour. Each day of competition covers a course. The course has specific start lines. The course has specific finish lines. The team with the shortest travel time wins. The travel time is cumulative. The ultimate goal of the Sun Rayce is to develop technologies. These technologies can be used in practical car applications.

Part B

Revise the paragraph by combining the ideas from the sentences in each group to write one new sentence. As you write each sentence, think about the emphasis and relationships you want to achieve, adding transition and linking words as needed.

1.

The Rayce is an unusual car race.

It is sponsored by the U.S. Energy Department, General Motors Corporation, and EDS.

It lasts ten days.

> EXAMPLE
>
> (Notice different ways to combine the sentences to change the emphasis.)
>
> *Lasting ten days, the Rayce is an unusual car race sponsored by the U.S. Energy Department, General Motors Corporation, and EDS.*
>
> **or**
>
> *Sponsored by the U.S. Energy Department, General Motors Corporation, and EDS, the ten-day Rayce is an unusual car race.*
>
> **or**
>
> *The Rayce, an unusual car race sponsored by the U.S. Energy Department, General Motors Corporation, and EDS, lasts ten days.*

2.

College teams build and drive their own solar race cars.

The cars are powered only by electricity from solar panels.

_____

_____

_____

_____

3.

To qualify for the race, the team's solar car must be able to travel a minimum of 125 miles.

The team's solar car must have a lap speed of at least 25 miles per hour.

_____

_____

_____

_____

4.

Each day of competition covers a course.

The course has specific start lines.

The course has specific finish lines.

_____

_____

_____

_____

5.

The team with the shortest travel time wins.

The travel time is cumulative.

_____

_____

_____

_____

6.

The ultimate goal of the Rayce is to develop technologies.

These technologies can be used in practical car applications.

_____

_____

_____

_____

Part C

After you have checked your sentences with your instructor, copy them to create a coherent paragraph. Note the differences between the original and the rewritten paragraphs.

Identify Sentences in Context

Run-on Sentences

To make meaning clear, you must show where sentences begin and end by using capital letters and end punctuation. When sentences are not separated correctly, the ideas are difficult to follow:

> The Indy 500 is the culmination of a month-long festival of motor racing during which 750,000 people go through the turnstiles on racing morning all lanes of traffic on every street and road leading to the track are filled with cars.

You probably had difficulty understanding the lines because what appears to be one sentence is actually two sentences punctuated as one. Without an end mark where it is needed, you don't know how to group the words to understand the thought. Sentences that run together can be fixed simply by adding a period at the end of the first sentence and a capital letter at the beginning of the second.

> The Indy 500 is the culmination of a month-long festival of motor racing during which 750,000 people go through the <u>turnstiles. On</u> racing morning, all lanes of traffic on every street and road leading to the track are filled with cars.

Sentence Fragments

Read some other mispunctuated sentences:

The turbocharger forces extra air into the engine. Increasing its power. The fastest "500" drivers attain speeds of 240 mph. Along the straightaways.

You may have had difficulty understanding the words because there are fragments of sentences punctuated as complete sentences. When you write, be on the lookout for parts of sentences that do not make sense by themselves. These fragments can be attached to a sentence that comes before or after the fragment, or they may be rewritten as a complete sentence. Corrected, the sentences would read as follows:

The turbocharger forces extra air into the engine, increasing its power. The fastest "500" drivers attain speeds of 240 mph along the straightaways.

The chart that follows summarizes ways to correct sentence fragments.

Clues to incomplete sentences	Examples of incomplete sentences	Complete sentences
Beginning with a word that ends with *-ing*	Racing around the corner.	*Racing around the corner,* the cyclist skidded.
Beginning with *because, although, if, while, when*	Because roads were inadequate.	*Because roads were inadequate,* driving was difficult.
Beginning with *which, that, who* (unless *who* or *which* begins a question)	That is televised.	The Indy 500 is a a race *that is televised.*
Containing a dropped word	The racer familiar with the course.	*The racer* was *familiar with the course.*
Beginning in the middle of a thought	So that we could see the game better.	We looked for seats *so that we could see the game better.*

In the next exercise you learn to recognize and punctuate complete sentences.

*One can never consent to creep when one feels
an impulse to soar.*

— Helen Keller (1880–1968)

EXERCISE 8   The Brickyard

The following paragraph about the Indy 500 is missing periods. Add a period to mark the end of a sentence and capitalize the beginning word of the next sentence. Copy on the adjacent numbered line each word you have capitalized.

The first Indianapolis 500 in 1911 marked the first long-distance auto race on a closed track often referred to as "The Brickyard," the 2.5-mile Indianapolis Motor Speedway was originally paved with 3.2 million bricks the USAC-CART "Indy-type" championship car can accelerate from 0 to 100 mph in four seconds the driver is strapped in almost flat on his back, wearing a fire-resistant suit and helmet at the first race in 1911 the auto industry leaders determined that there were too many cars for a standing start they decided it was safer to lead the cars around with a passenger car and release them with a flag since then a pace car has always been used for mass rolling starts.

1. _____
2. _____
3. _____
4. _____
5. _____
6. _____
7. _____
8. _____
9. _____
10. _____
11. _____
12. _____
13. _____

Rearrange and Combine Sentences Using Transitions

In the next exercise you will decide which sentences to arrange and combine to create a paragraph. The skills you develop will help you revise your own writing.

As you decide what ideas to combine, it is important to know some techniques for punctuating sentences.

METHODS FOR PUNCTUATING SENTENCES

Add . . .	Sentence example
a period	The 1936 Indy 500 winner, Louis Meyer, was photographed drinking his favorite beverage, buttermilk, after his <u>victory**.** From</u> that year on, the American Dairy Association made sure that the winner of the race received a bottle of milk.
a semicolon	The 1936 Indy 500 winner, Louis Meyer, was photographed drinking his favorite beverage, buttermilk, after his <u>victory**;** from</u> that year on, the American Dairy Association made sure that the winner of the race received a bottle of milk.
a connecting word after a semicolon	The 1936 Indy 500 winner, Louis Meyer, was photographed drinking his favorite beverage, buttermilk, after his <u>victory</u>**; in fact,** from that year on, the American Dairy Association made sure that the winner of the race received a bottle of milk.
and/but/or/for/so/yet after a comma	The 1936 Indy 500 winner, Louis Meyer, was photographed drinking his favorite beverage, buttermilk, after his <u>victory**, so**</u> from that year on, the American Dairy Association made sure that the winner of the race received a bottle of milk.

Note: Two sentences are not correctly joined with a comma alone.

*There are no speed limits on the road
to success.*

— David W. Johnson

EXERCISE 9 Finding the Finish Line

Part A

Read a draft of an informative paragraph about road rallies. In Parts B and C you will work on combining, rearranging, and adding transitions to make the paragraph coherent.

A road rally is not a race. A road rally is a competition usually driven on public roads. A road rally is completed at or below legal speeds. A road rally requires some equipment. A pencil is needed. Some paper is needed. A timekeeping device measuring seconds is needed. A roadworthy vehicle seating a two-person team is needed. One person is the driver. The other person is the navigator. The navigator receives instructions. The instructions detail the route of the race. The instructions detail the speed the car should travel. The navigator gives instructions to the driver. On the route are checkpoints. Checkpoints are timing stations. Penalty points are given to teams that arrive at checkpoints too early. Penalty points are given to teams that arrive at checkpoints too late. The team drives from checkpoint to checkpoint. The team completes the race. The team that has the fewest number of penalty points is the winner. A team does not win a road rally by driving the fastest. A team wins a road rally by driving the smartest.

Part B

Revise the paragraph by using rearrangement and combining wherever appropriate to create new sentences. Not every sentence needs to be rewritten. The first few sentences are combined for you.

Sentences 1–3 are combined.

1. A road rally is not a race.

2. A road rally is a competition usually driven on public roads.

3. A road rally is completed at or below legal speeds

    A road rally is not a race but a competition driven on public roads at or below legal speeds.

Sentence 4 is not combined.

4. A road rally requires some equipment.

Sentences 5–8 are combined.

5. A pencil is needed.

6. Some paper is needed.

7. A timekeeping device measuring seconds is needed.

8. A roadworthy vehicle seating a two-person team is needed.

   In addition to a pencil, some paper, and a timekeeping device measuring seconds, a roadworthy vehicle seating a two-person team is needed.

Now continue to revise the sentences by rearranging and combining to create new sentences.

9. One person is the driver.

10. The other person is the navigator.

11. The navigator receives instructions.

12. The instructions detail the route of the race.

13. The instructions detail the speed the car should travel.

14. The navigator gives instructions to the driver.

15. On the route are checkpoints.

16. Checkpoints are timing stations.

17. Penalty points are given to teams that arrive at checkpoints too early.

18. Penalty points are given to teams that arrive at checkpoints too late.

19. The team drives from checkpoint to checkpoint.

20. The team completes the race.

21. The team that has the fewest number of penalty points is the winner.

22. A team does not win a road rally by driving the fastest.

23. A team wins a road rally by driving the smartest.

Part C

After you have checked your sentences with your instructor, copy them to create a paragraph. Note the differences between the original and the rewritten paragraphs.

How to Write a Paragraph

In this section you are asked to write an 8-to-12-sentence paragraph about what you know, based on your experiences, memories, and current thoughts. Suppose, for example, you were to write about the following topic:

> Just as the drivers in the 1908 auto race participated in a new beginning in racing competition, you, too, may have experienced a new beginning—at school, at home, or at work. Write about a new beginning you have had.

Questions to Consider

What was the new beginning?

When and where did it happen?

Why was the new beginning significant to you?

How do you feel about what happened?

What process can you use to write a paragraph?

• First, make a list of ideas that you could use in your writing. Quickly, without much thought, write anything that comes to mind so that you have some ideas on paper to think about.

>   **Beginnings?**
>   ```
>   school—elementary, trade school, college
>   family—new brother-in-law
>   new house
>   new job
>   ```

- Make your list as long as you can. Then, go back to check what is interesting. You may want to write a new list related to that idea. You may need to make several more lists to capture the ideas you want to use in your paragraph.

> **New Job?**
>
> ```
> this past spring
>
> at the mall
>
> work as sales associate
>
> never did that work before
>
> had training
>
> pay not too good
>
> other workers are friendly
>
> work as many hours as I can
> ```

- When you have some ideas, answer the questions that are suggested for developing your paragraph. Answering these questions helps you organize your ideas.

> **What was the new beginning?** `I worked at the sporting goods store.`
>
> **When and where did it happen?** `I began there last spring.`
>
> **Why was the new beginning significant to you?** `The work was hard because I never did store work before. I had training classes. I learned what it was like to work in a store, organize the merchandise, use the computer, help the customers.`
>
> **How do you feel about what happened?** `I am glad I left washing cars to work at the store, even though I don't make much more money. I learned a lot. I made new friends. I still work there.`

- Then, write a first draft of your paragraph.

Topic Sentence

Begin your paragraph with a topic sentence. **A topic sentence has the job of both stating the topic and providing a reaction to the topic.** You can use an idea from your list or an answer to one of the **Questions to Consider** to help you write this sentence. Your topic and reaction must be limited in scope so that it can be developed in a single paragraph. What makes an effective topic sentence? Consider the following examples.

> I started a job.

This topic sentence is **weak.** Although there is a topic "a job," the topic is too broad to develop in a single paragraph.

> I started a job at a sporting goods store recently.

This topic sentence is stronger than the first one because the addition of the words "at a sporting goods store recently" limits the discussion of the topic, but the sentence does not provide a reaction to the topic.

> I recently experienced a positive new beginning by taking a job at a sporting goods store.

This sentence is an **effective topic sentence.** The addition of the words "positive new beginning" provides a reaction that focuses the paragraph.

Draft of Middle or Body Sentences

The middle or body sentences explain or support your topic sentences. When you include specific details, you help the reader understand your ideas.

I got the job and began work at the store last spring. The work was hard because I never did store work before. Fortunately, they have a good training program. I had a chance to go to classes and watch videos and read training manuals. Other employees helped me. I learned what it was like to work in a store. I learned to organize the merchandise. My responsibility is usually the training machines, like the stationary bicycles and outdoor wear. I learned to use the computer. I use the computer to make charges and check inventory. I like to help the customers. They always have questions. Now that I have been at the store a while, I can answer most of the questions.

Draft of a Concluding Sentence

The purpose of the concluding sentence is to bring your paragraph to an end and let your reader know you are finished. Your answers to the last question give you ideas about how to finish your paragraph.

```
    I am glad I left washing cars to work at the store
even though I don't make much more money. I learned a
lot. I made new friends. I still work there.
```

Draft of a Paragraph

```
    I recently experienced a positive new beginning at
a sporting goods store. I got the job and began work
at the store last spring. The work was hard because
I never did store work before. They have a good
training program. I had a chance to go to classes
and watch videos and read training manuals. Other
employees helped me. I learned what it was like to
work in a store. I learned to organize the
merchandise. My responsibility is usually the
training machines, like the stationary bicycles
and outdoor wear. I learned to use the computer. I
use the computer to make charges and check inventory.
I like to help the customers. They always have
questions. Now that I have been at the store a while,
I can answer most of the questions. I am glad I left
washing cars to work at the store even though I don't
make much more money. I learned a lot. I made new
friends. I still work there.
```

Now, work on your draft to be sure you have

- A clear topic sentence

    Does the topic sentence state the topic?

    Does the topic sentence state what you will tell about the topic?

- Convincing support

    Do your sentences say what you want them to mean?

    Have you included enough details to make your ideas clear?

- Effective Organization

    Does the paragraph have a beginning, a middle, and an end?

    Does your concluding sentence provide a summary of your main idea?

    Do you use transitions to link your ideas?

- Successful sentences

    Is each sentence complete?

    Have you eliminated run-ons and fragments?

    Have you written each word you need?

    Have you used a spell checker, speller, or dictionaries to be sure words are spelled correctly? Have you used the correct form of homonyms?

    The Language Supplement provides help in creating error-free sentences.

- Effective title

    Does your title suggest what the paragraph is about and make someone interested in reading what you have written?

Use a word processor to type your paper and read it one more time to complete the process of writing a paragraph.

Rewritten Draft

NEW BEGINNING AT THE SPORTING GOODS STORE

I recently experienced a positive new beginning by taking a job at a sporting goods store. I interviewed for the job last spring and began work the next week. The work was hard since I had never done it before. Management, however, provided me with an excellent training program. In addition to going to classes, watching training videos, and reading training manuals, I had the other employees to help me. Quickly, it seemed, I learned what it is like to work in a store. One of my main responsibilities is organizing the merchandise, usually the training machines, like the stationary bicycles and outdoor wear. Since I have learned how to use the computer, I make charges and check inventory. What is most fun is answering the customers' questions. Now that I have been at the store a while, I can answer most of their inquiries. Working with sporting goods, I am learning a lot and making friends with employees and customers. Even though I don't make much more money, I am glad I left washing cars to work at the store.

Notice how the underlined words in the rewritten draft make the paragraph easy to read. Words that link sentences together are called transitions.

Transitions

Transition can be achieved in a variety of ways.

Technique #1

Repeat a word or group of words from the first sentence in the second sentence.

> I recently experienced a positive new beginning by taking a job at a sporting goods store.

> I interviewed for the job last spring and began work the next week.

Technique #2

Use another word that is a synonym or means the same as a word in the first sentence.

> What is most fun is answering the customers' questions.

> Now that I have been at the store a while, I can answer most of their inquiries.

Technique #3

Use a transition word.

> Management, however, provided me with an excellent training program.

> In addition to going to classes, watching videos, and reading training manuals, I had the other employees to help me.

> Even though I don't make much more money, I am glad I left washing cars to work at the store.

TRANSITION WORD CHART

To show addition	also, next, another, and, in addition, moreover, further, furthermore, finally, besides, and then, likewise, nor, too, again, equally important, last, incidentally
To show contrast	but, yet, however, still, nevertheless, on the other hand, on the contrary, even so, in contrast to
To show similarity	like, likewise, similarly
To show time order	first, then, next, after, as, before, while, meanwhile, soon, now, during, finally, subsequently, at the same time
To show space order	here, beyond, nearby, below, opposite to, adjacent to, on the opposite side of, nearby, across, to the left, to the right, next
To show a relationship of cause and effect	therefore, consequently, as a result
To show emphasis	indeed, in fact, without a doubt
To show illustration	for example, for instance, that is, in other words, specifically, such as
To show summary or clarification	in summary, in conclusion, in brief, after all

Writing from Experience

EXERCISE 10   Write a Paragraph

Write a paragraph of 8–12 sentences on one of the following topics.

1. Just as the drivers in the 1908 auto race participated in a new beginning in racing competition, you, too, may have experienced a new beginning—at school, at home, or at work. Write about a new beginning you have had.

    Questions to Consider

    What was the new beginning?

    When and where did it happen?

    Why was the new beginning significant to you?

    How do you feel about what happened?

2. Auto racing involves both participants as well as spectators. Write about a time when you were either a participant in or a spectator at any type of competition.

    Questions to Consider

    What type of competition did you participate in or watch?

    When and where did the competition take place?

    Describe the sights and sounds.

    Did the competition conclude as you had hoped? Why or why not?

3. Many activities involve a great deal of teamwork. Write about an experience working with a team.

    Questions to Consider

    What was the purpose of the team?

    When and where were you involved working with a team?

    Why were you working with this team?

    Who were the others on the team?

    Was the teamwork effective or ineffective? Why?

4. Auto racing involves overcoming obstacles. Write about an experience when you overcame an obstacle.

    Questions to Consider

    What was the obstacle?

    When and where were you?

    Did you work through the challenge yourself? Did others help you?

    When did you overcome the obstacle?

    How do you feel about the experience now?

For question 5, you are on your own to decide a focus and to create questions for development.

5. When people have more demands on their time than time, life can seem like a race. Tell about an experience when you felt you had to race, not literally but figuratively, from one place or task to another.

    Questions for Development

    _____

    _____

    _____

    _____

For question 6, you are on your own to decide a focus and to create questions for development.

6. Write on a topic of your choice about automobiles.

    Focus

    _____

    Questions for Development

    _____

    _____

    _____

    _____

EXERCISE 11   Revise Your Paragraph

Part A

Reread the paragraph you wrote for Exercise 10.

1. Choose one sentence to rearrange.

    Original Sentence _____

    _____

    Rearranged Sentence _____

    _____

2. Choose two or more sentences that could be effectively combined.

    Original Sentences

    _____

    _____

    _____

    _____

    Combined Sentences

    _____

    _____

    _____

You may want to use these revised sentences in the final draft of your paragraph.

Part B

Check your paragraph before submitting your final draft.

CLEAR TOPIC SENTENCE

❒   Does the topic sentence state the topic?

❒   Does the topic sentence state what you will tell about the topic?

CONVINCING SUPPORT

❐ Do your sentences say what you want them to mean?

❐ Have you included enough details to make your ideas clear?

EFFECTIVE ORGANIZATION

❐ Does the paragraph have a beginning, a middle, and an end?

❐ Does your concluding sentence provide a summary of your main idea?

❐ Do you use transitions to link your ideas?

SUCCESSFUL SENTENCES

❐ Is each sentence complete?

❐ Have you eliminated run-ons and fragments?

❐ Have you written each word you need?

❐ Have you used a spell checker, speller, or dictionary to be sure words are spelled correctly?

❐ Have you used the correct form of homonyms?

EFFECTIVE TITLE

❐ Does your title suggest what the paragraph is about and make someone interested in reading it?

The final section of this chapter gives you additional opportunity to read and write as you learn more about the chapter topic. As you know, reading and writing work together. When you read to answer the questions, you expand your knowledge base so that you have more to write about. In addition, as you read, you become increasingly familiar with sentence structure and style.

Writing from Resources

EXERCISE 12   Share Information

To answer these questions, visit a library or use a search engine on the Internet, such as Lycos, Yahoo, or AltaVista. As you write your answers, use sentence rearrangement and combining techniques.

Your instructor will explain how to complete this section regarding the number of questions to answer and whether to work independently, with a partner, or in a group.

Cow Pastures and Sandy Beaches

1. How is a stock car different from and yet similar to a car off the assembly line?

California Hot Wheels

2. What are the challenges of drag racing?

Powered by the Sun

3. What was the course of the most recent Sun Rayce? What did the winning vehicle look like?

4. How does a solar car operate without gasoline?

The Brickyard

5. Why did operating the early Indy 500 race cars require more than one person?

6. In addition to the Indy 500, what other races take place at the Brickyard?

Finding the Finish Line

7. What are the challenges of driving a rally race?

8. What is international rallying? In what countries are the major rallies held?

More About Auto Racing

9. Of the cars that started the 1908 auto race from New York to Paris, which cars made it to Paris? Why didn't the German car finish in first place even though it was the first car to arrive at Paris?

10. What is midget car racing?

11. What is go-cart racing?

12. What is a gymkhana?

EXERCISE 13   Understand Idioms

Idioms are groups of words that, taken together, have a special meaning. Using these idioms can make informal language colorful and descriptive. Finding the meaning of idioms, however, can take some practice. Since an idiom is a phrase or group of words that has meaning as a unit, knowing the meaning of each individual word will not give you the meaning of the idiom. To find the meaning, check a dictionary or a specialized idiom dictionary, or ask someone who understands the idiom to explain it to you.

What is the meaning of each of the following idioms related to automobiles?

inside track

when the rubber hits the road

backseat driver

blow your own horn

floor it

spinning your wheels

pit stop

put on the gas

put your pedal to the metal

explore every avenue

race against time

CHAPTER 2

Food

Eating is not merely a material pleasure. Eating well gives a spectacular joy to life and contributes immensely to goodwill and happy companionship. It is of great importance to the morale.

— Elsa Schiaparelli (1890–1973)

In matters of cuisine, even typically mild-mannered people generally have strong opinions about what is delicious and what is inedible. In the reading in this chapter you will read about favorite foods during past decades.

Connecting Reading with Writing

EXERCISE 1   Reflections on Food

1. Describe one of your favorite meals.

    _____

    _____

    _____

2. How many meals have you eaten away from home this past week? Why did you eat out rather than at home?

    _____

    _____

    _____

    _____

Bananas-Popcorn-and-Mayonnaise Salad?

by Marty Meitus

1   Bananas-popcorn-and-mayonnaise salad was one of the worst combos to come out of the 1920s. But pineapple upside-down cake was also of the era, and some of us are still making it. Just as fashion changes with the decades—and may produce hip huggers with wide belts and white boots—so it is with food.

2   Here is a decade-by-decade look at food trends from Sylvia Lovegren, author of *Fashionable Food,* and Bonnie Bailey, author of a dessert

retrospective[1] for Eagle Brand sweetened condensed milk, starting in the 1920s because the end of World War I was the beginning of the modern kitchen era:

- 1920s—Salads cupped in a lettuce leaf, tomato aspic and gelatin salads, frozen fruit salads, tea rooms, chicken à la king on toast points, puddings (including vanilla-banana-Nilla wafer pudding), icebox cakes, canned crushed pineapple, marshmallows (as an ingredient), Lady Baltimore cake. The jazz age brought candy shops and chocolate emporiums[2] on every corner and a propensity[3] for fudge.
- 1930s—What was hot? Marshmallows in non-sweet dishes, notably a sweet potato and marshmallow concoction, Sunday night suppers for friends and families, creamed chipped beef, chili con carne, tea parties, club luncheons, grilled cheese sandwiches with tomato and bacon, and gingerbread. The Depression years brought some pretty grim foods, such as turnips au gratin, as people tried to stretch the budget. Canned foods, popularized in the '20s, filtered into the '30s. Often recipes would call for one canned food on top of another. Entertaining consisted of chafing dish sorts of foods, popularizing dishes such as Welsh rarebit. The '30s homemakers also had a penchant[4] for making something look like something else, as in the surprise sandwich, which featured three layers of stuffed bread, frosted with cream cheese to look like a cake. Cobblers and fruit pies were popular because they could be stretched to feed a crowd.
- 1940s—Meatloaf, noodle or rice rings filled with creamed chicken or other proteins, Swiss steak, chocolate chip cookies, chiffon cakes, hot fudge pudding cake, coffee-and-dessert parties, Victory gardens, progressive parties (where guests traveled from home to home for each course), potluck suppers, pumpkin pie.

The government came out with its recommended daily allowances in 1941, setting the tone for the decade, as everyone tried to get enough nutrients to "build strong bodies." The original basic seven food groups (butter and fortified margarine were considered a

[1] **retrospective** presentation, showcase
[2] **emporium** store, shop
[3] **propensity** inclination, tendency
[4] **penchant** fondness, liking

food group) was eventually modified to the basic four and replaced in the '90s with the food pyramid.

Resourceful cooks stretched limited resources with noodle rings filled with creamed protein, including a grits ring filled with creamed cod. Elaborate desserts were simplified as women went to work to support the war effort. Cake mixes and biscuit mixes came into vogue[5] because they required few additional (and possibly rationed) ingredients. To stretch the use of chocolate, marble cakes that required a small amount of chocolate swirled in the batter also came into vogue.

- 1950s—Steak, beef stroganoff, Jell-O molds, three bean salad, gourmet cooking, clam dip, fruit cocktail, Spam, kebabs, Swedish meatballs, cheese balls rolled in pecans, casseroles, cocktail parties, suburban barbecues, TV mix (Cheerios, Rice Chex, pretzels, peanuts, garlic salt, and Accent), baked Alaska. Steak became the archetypal[6] '50s food as Americans were told to eat lots of protein.

- 1960s—Julia Child, the Kennedys and their French chef, beef Wellington, chocolate mousse, flambéed[7] desserts, green beans amadine, fondues, Spanish Mediterranean (gazpacho, paella), gooey desserts, cheesecake, cherry cheese pie, rum balls, grass-hopper pie, health foods (often pseudo health foods), soul foods.

  French cooking was the hallmark of the early part of the decade; anything Julia Child cooked on television became an instant success. But as the Age of Aquarius dawned, health food advocates[8] began to do battle with the establishment, worried about chemical fertilizers and pesticides in their food. However, without as many food resources and with scant information for their cause, much of the early cooking was tasteless and extreme—and even potentially problematic as with fitness guru[9] Adelle Davis' raw unpasteurized milk "health" shakes.

- 1970s—Brunch, crepes, pasta with creamy white sauces, anything with a cute name as Harvey Wallbangers, salad bars, granola, wacky or crazy cake, rum bundt cakes, lemon bars, magic cookie bars, early nouvelle cuisine (terrines, coulis), early California cuisine.

---

[5] **vogue**   fashion, style

[6] **archetypal**   model, representative

[7] **flambéed**   served flaming

[8] **advocates**   supporters, promoters

[9] **guru**   teacher, counselor

Young baby boomers were setting the trend, says Lovegren. "There was a lot of rich, sweet kid food, such as butter pecan extravaganzas . . . Everything had cream, sour cream, sugar, shredded cheese. It wasn't real grown-up food until nouvelle cuisine came along."

- 1980s—California cuisine (light sauces, fresh ingredients), baby vegetables, fish and seafood, roasted red peppers, designer pizzas, Cajun food, Vietnamese, grazing, tapas, croissants, muffins, comfort food, teas, tomato salsas, Southwestern cuisine, premium ice creams, frozen yogurt.

The yuppie age brought a kind of frenetic[10] quality to the era. "People would jog over to my gourmet food shop," says Bailey, "and eat four cookies." Everything new was considered better, whether it was a salad of field greens or a purple potato.

- 1990s—Lowfat, Italian cooking, fusion cooking, fruit salsas, chutneys, curries, habañero chiles, beans, grains, pasta, rotisserie chicken, bagels, Thai, vegetarian, organics, olive oil, balsamic vinegar, cultivated "wild" mushrooms, cappuccino, lattes, espressos.

3   Lovegren is a little concerned at the direction we've taken in the '90s— fast food, gourmet take-out and the decline of the home-cooked meal, and she predicts much of the same in the coming decades. "I think we're getting so far away from home cooking now, and the number of people who cook nowadays is so small; I think the conclusion is that in 50 years, cooking will be for the extremely poor or for the hobbyist. The rest of us will be getting food from other people who make it, expensive charcuteries, fast food."

EXERCISE 2   Questions About the Reading

Select the letter that best completes each question or statement.

1.   The passage focuses mainly on

   A.   healthful snacks.

   B.   unusual menus.

   C.   popular foods.

   D.   home cooking.

[10] **frenetic**   wild, chaotic

2. Choose the sentence that tells the main idea.

    A. The number of people who cook nowadays is so small; I think the conclusion is that in 50 years, cooking will be for the extremely poor or for the hobbyist.

    B. Here is a decade-by-decade look at food trends starting in the 1920s because the end of World War I was the beginning of the modern kitchen era.

    C. The government came out with its recommended daily allowances in 1941, setting the tone for the decade, as everyone tried to get enough nutrients to "build strong bodies."

    D. Without as many food resources and with scant information for their cause, much of the early cooking was tasteless and extreme.

3. Before the food pyramid was developed,

    A. people were unconcerned about nutrients.

    B. four basic food groups had been identified.

    C. there were no daily food allowances.

    D. few people were eating home-cooked meals.

4. The last paragraph leads us to believe that

    A. increasing numbers of people are eating away from home.

    B. cooking at home is a necessity for most people.

    C. a majority of Americans cook at home as a hobby.

    D. few people today work away from home as cooks.

5. The author mentions *turnips au gratin* to show that

    A. people in the 1930s liked to eat vegetables, especially turnips.

    B. turnips are a healthful vegetable, especially when served with cheese.

    C. the name given to a food dish can make it popular.

    D. people can be creative even when they are economizing.

6. As used in the sentence "The rest of us will be getting food from other people who make it, expensive *charcuteries,* fast food," *charcuteries* means

   A. pizza places.

   B. hot dog stands.

   C. delicatessens.

   D. cafeterias.

EXERCISE 3   Sentence Explication

1. Either use the sentence that follows, or select and copy a different sentence from the reading selection.

   I think the conclusion is that in 50 years, cooking will be for the extremely poor or for the hobbyist.

   paragraph #3

   Or the sentence you choose:

   _____

   _____

   _____

   paragraph #___

2. Paraphrase the sentence by rewriting it in your own words.

   _____

   _____

   _____

3. React to the sentence. What comments and questions do you have about it?

    _____

    _____

    _____

4. Relate to the sentence. What personal experiences does it bring to mind?

    _____

    _____

    _____

    _____

    _____

    _____

    _____

EXERCISE 4   Questions for Writing and Discussion

1. Where did the author find information about food trends over the years?

2. How did events or developments in the United States influence the cuisine? Give at least three examples.

3. What are some concerns about current food trends?

Working from Sentences to Paragraph

Rearrange Sentences with New Beginnings

---

*Food probably has a very great influence on
the condition of men. Who knows if a
well-prepared soup was responsible for the
pneumatic pump or a poor soup for a war?*

— G. C. Lichtenberg

EXERCISE 5   Soup's On

Part A

Use the provided new sentence beginnings to change the emphasis of the following sentences that describe one of America's first fast foods. As you rearrange the words, be sure to keep the meaning of the original sentence.

1.   A person who helped change the eating habits of Americans in the early 1900s was Dr. John Thompson Dorrance, a chemist working at the Joseph Campbell Preserve Company.

   In the early 1900s, _____

   _____

   _____

2.   Twenty-one varieties of high quality, tasty condensed soup selling at just ten cents a can were created by the Campbell Company under his direction.

   Under his direction, the Campbell Company _____

   _____

   _____

3. Tomato, chicken, oxtail, pea, mock turtle, asparagus, and tomato okra soup were some of the most popular soups.

   Some of the most popular soups were _____

   _____

   _____

4. A person could prepare an inexpensive meal for the family simply by adding a can of hot water and stirring.

   To prepare _____

   _____

   _____

5. The classic red-and-white soup-can label was inspired by the uniforms of the Cornell College football team.

   The uniforms of the Cornell College football team _____

   _____

   _____

6. An award from the 1900 Paris Exposition is represented by the gold medal on the label.

   The gold medal on the label _____

   _____

   _____

7. A classic pop-art painting paying tribute to the tomato soup can brought considerable acclaim to Andy Warhol, a famous artist.

   Andy Warhol _____

   _____

   _____

8. Dorrance died in 1930, at age 56, and at that time he was the third richest man in the United States.

At the time _____

_____

_____

Part B

After checking your rearranged sentences with your instructor, copy them to create a paragraph.

Combine Sentences with New Beginnings

*Just a spoonful of sugar makes the medicine
go down in a most delightful way.*

— Mary Poppins

EXERCISE 6   Sweet, Sticky, Fat-Free Goo

Part A

Read the following draft of an informative paragraph about one of the world's oldest confections. In Parts B and C, you will work on combining sentences and adding transitions to make the paragraph coherent.

In ancient Egypt, marshmallows were made from the marshmallow root. Marshmallows were a special treat. In France in the mid-1800s, owners of candy stores made marshmallows. The owners made marshmallows by hand. Candy makers needed to make marshmallows quickly. Candy makers began to use molds. Nineteenth-century candy makers replaced mallow root with gelatin. Nineteenth-century candy makers added corn syrup, cornstarch, and sugar. The "extrusion process" was discovered in the mid-twentieth century. The mixed ingredients were piped through long tubes. The mixed ingredients were cut into equal pieces. Marshmallows were cooked. Marshmallows were formed. Marshmallows were bagged. This took 60 minutes. Marshmallows are popular with Americans. Americans purchase more than 95 million pounds annually.

Part B

Combine the ideas from the sentences in each group to write one new sentence. Begin the new sentence using the indicated words. As you write each sentence, think about the emphasis and relationships you want to achieve.

1.

In ancient Egypt, marshmallows were made from the marshmallow root.

Marshmallows were a special treat.

Marshmallows _____

_____

_____

_____

2.

In France in the mid-1800s, owners of candy stores made marshmallows.

The owners made marshmallows by hand.

French candy store owners _____

_____

_____

_____

3.

Candy makers needed to make marshmallows quickly.

Candy makers began to use molds.

Because they _____

_____

_____

_____

4.

Nineteenth-century candy makers replaced mallow root with gelatin.

Nineteenth-century candy makers added corn syrup, cornstarch, and sugar.

To make marshmallows _____

_____

_____

_____

5.

The "extrusion process" was discovered in the mid-twentieth century.

The mixed ingredients were piped through long tubes.

The mixed ingredients were cut into equal pieces.

In the "extrusion process" _____

_____

_____

_____

6.

Marshmallows were cooked.

Marshmallows were formed.

Marshmallows were bagged.

This took 60 minutes.

In 60 minutes _____

_____

_____

7.

Marshmallows are popular with Americans.

Americans purchase more than 95 million pounds annually.

Marshmallows _____

_____

_____

Part C

After checking your combined sentences with your instructor, copy them to create a paragraph. Add transitions and linking words to make the paragraph coherent. Note the differences between the original and the rewritten paragraphs.

Combine Sentences on Your Own

Put your hand on a hot stove for a minute, and it seems like an hour. Sit with a pretty girl for an hour, and it seems like a minute.

— Albert Einstein (1879–1955)

EXERCISE 7 Popcorn

Part A

Read the following draft paragraph about a popular snack. In Parts B and C, you will work on combining sentences and adding transitions to make the paragraph coherent.

This happened at the end of the nineteenth century. Popcorn became very popular. The Sears Roebuck catalogue advertised sacks of popping corn. The sacks weighed 25 pounds. The sacks cost one dollar each. Storing large quantities of corn was a problem. Kernels dried out. Kernels didn't pop. Unpopped kernels were called duds. Unpopped kernels were called "old maids." In the 1930s, popcorn was inexpensive. It cost 5 or 10 cents a bag. During World War II, there was a shortage of sugar to make candy. Americans began eating three times more popcorn than before the war. In 1945, Percy Spencer made a discovery. He discovered what happened when popcorn was placed under microwave energy. The popcorn popped. A survey taken during the mid-fifties showed that television viewers enjoyed popcorn. Viewers ate popcorn as often as four nights a week. This occurred by the end of the twentieth century. Popcorn was a favorite snack food. The average American consumed about 68 quarts a year.

Part B

Revise the paragraph by combining the ideas from the sentences in each group to write one new sentence. As you write each sentence, think about the emphasis and relationships you want to achieve, adding transition and linking words as needed.

1.

This happened at the end of the nineteenth century.

Popcorn became very popular.

_____

_____

_____

_____

2.

The Sears Roebuck catalogue advertised sacks of popping corn.

The sacks weighed 25 pounds.

The sacks cost one dollar each.

_____

_____

_____

_____

3.

Storing large quantities of corn was a problem.

Kernels dried out.

Kernels didn't pop.

_____

_____

_____

_____

4.

Unpopped kernels were called duds.

Unpopped kernels were called "old maids."

_____

_____

_____

_____

5.

In the 1930s, popcorn was inexpensive.
It cost 5 or 10 cents a bag.

_____

_____

_____

_____

6.

During World War II, there was a shortage of sugar to make candy.
Americans began eating three times more popcorn than before the war.

_____

_____

_____

_____

7.

In 1945, Percy Spencer made a discovery.
He discovered what happened when popcorn was placed under microwave energy.
The popcorn popped.

_____

_____

_____

_____

8.

A survey taken during the 1950s showed that television viewers enjoyed popcorn.
Television viewers ate popcorn as often as four nights a week.

_____

_____

_____

_____

9.

This occurred by the end of the twentieth century.

Popcorn was a favorite snack food.

The average American consumed about 68 quarts a year.

_____

_____

_____

_____

Part C

After you have checked your sentences with your instructor, copy them to create a coherent paragraph. Note the differences between the original and the rewritten paragraphs.

_____

*If you are planning for a year, sow rice; if you
are planning for a decade, plant trees; if you
are planning for a lifetime, educate people.*

— Chinese proverb

_____

Identify Sentences in Context

EXERCISE 8 Versatile Rice

The following paragraph about a popular grain is missing periods. Add a period to mark the end of a sentence and capitalize the beginning word of the next sentence. Copy on the adjacent numbered line each word you have capitalized.

"Have you eaten your rice today?" is an appropriate everyday greeting for some Asian Americans at the beginning of a new year an equally appropriate wish is "May your rice never burn!" rice consumption has more than doubled in the United States since 1972 one explanation is an interest in rice for improving diet and health another reason is an increase in the numbers of Asian and Hispanic people, who often prefer rice to other cereal foods rice is served in various ways for breakfast, lunch, and dinner it can be part of an appetizer, main course, or dessert brown rice is more nutritious than polished white rice, but it is less popular many people think white rice is tastier and easier to cook various types of rice are grown in level, well-prepared fields although not scientifically proven effective, rice is believed to have medicinal benefits, such as in aiding digestion, increasing appetite, and curing indigestion.

1. _____
2. _____
3. _____
4. _____
5. _____
6. _____
7. _____
8. _____
9. _____
10. _____
11. _____
12. _____
13. _____
14. _____
15. _____
16. _____
17. _____
18. _____

Rearrange and Combine Sentences Using Transitions

> *Tomatoes and oregano make it Italian; wine*
> *and tarragon make it French. Sour cream*
> *makes it Russian; lemon and cinnamon make*
> *it Greek. Soy sauce makes it Chinese;*
> *garlic makes it good.*
>
> — Alice May Brock

EXERCISE 9   Garlic—The Stinking Rose

Part A

Read a draft of an informative paragraph about an herb with medicinal value. In Parts B and C, you will work on combining, rearranging, and adding transitions to make the paragraph coherent.

A bumper sticker had a message. "Eat garlic—It's Chic to Reek" was what it said. Garlic *(allium sativum)* is a member of the lily family. Garlic is a close relative of the onion. Garlic contains sulfur compounds. The compounds give garlic a pungent, spicy aroma. People may not want to get close to someone who has consumed raw garlic. Garlic has healing properties. Eating garlic can lower blood pressure. Eating garlic can reduce cholesterol. Over the years, garlic has been used for many treatments. Garlic was used to treat toothache and earache. Garlic was used to treat snakebite, whooping cough, and baldness. Some people don't like the smell of garlic. These people can use garlic in a dry or tablet form.

Part B

Revise the paragraph by using rearrangement, combining, and transitions *wherever appropriate* to create new sentences. Not every sentence needs to be rewritten.

1. A bumper sticker had a message.

2. "Eat garlic—It's Chic to Reek" was what it said.

3. Garlic *(allium sativum)* is a member of the lily family.

4. Garlic is a close relative of the onion.

5. Garlic contains sulfur compounds.

6. The compounds give garlic a pungent, spicy aroma.

7. People may not want to get close to someone who has consumed raw garlic.

8. Garlic has healing properties.

9. Eating garlic can lower blood pressure.

10. Eating garlic can reduce cholesterol.

11. Over the years, garlic has been used for many treatments.

12. Garlic was used to treat toothache and earache.

13. Garlic was used to treat snakebite, whooping cough, and baldness.

14. Some people don't like the smell of garlic.

15. These people can use garlic in a dry or tablet form.

Part C

After you have checked your sentences with your instructor, copy them to create a paragraph. Note the differences between the original and the rewritten paragraphs.

Writing from Experience

EXERCISE 10 Write a Paragraph

Write a paragraph of 8–12 sentences on one of the following topics.

1. Meals that are part of a festive event can be meaningful, but any mealtime can be memorable whether or not its purpose is to celebrate a special occasion. Tell about a meal you have especially enjoyed.

    Questions to Consider

    When did the meal take place?

    What was the occasion?

    Where did the meal take place?

    Who was at the meal?

    What was served?

    Why was the meal memorable?

2. Not only the taste but the sight, smell, and texture can influence your reaction to food. Choose a food that either appeals to you or repulses you. Describe how this food affects your senses.

    Questions to Consider

    What is the food?

    What is your reaction to it?

    How does it look?

    How does it smell?

    If you hold or touch the food, how does it feel?

    How does the food taste?

    On what occasions or how often do you eat the food?

3.   Although most meals are fairly routine, over the years it is quite possible that some occasion has been unique. This meal may have been one of a kind because of a single factor such as setting, menu, or companions. Or, the meal may be memorable for a variety of reasons. Tell about one of the most *unusual* meals you have ever had.

Questions to Consider

What made the meal unusual?

When was the meal?

Where was the meal?

Who was at the meal?

What foods/beverages were served?

What was your reaction to the occasion?

Would you repeat the experience?

4.   Some say a good cook is born with talent; others say a good cook has had a good teacher. Whatever the source of the skill, a person who prepares delicious food is a person to be appreciated. Tell about the good cook you are or about a good cook you know.

Questions to Consider

Who is the cook?

What does this person cook especially well?

What is good about the food?

Does this person enjoy cooking? Why or why not?

For question 5, you are on your own to create questions for development.

5. You may be one of the many Americans who eat out in restaurants. If so, you probably have favorites. Tell what makes one of your favorite restaurants a good place to eat.

Questions for Development

_____

_____

_____

_____

_____

For question 6, you are on your own to decide a focus and to create questions for development.

6. Write on a topic of your choice related to food.

Focus

_____

Questions for Development

_____

_____

_____

_____

EXERCISE 11   Revise Your Paragraph

Reread the paragraph you wrote for Exercise 10.

Part A

1. Choose one sentence to rearrange.

    Original Sentence _____

    _____

    Rearranged Sentence _____

    _____

2. Choose two or more sentences that could be effectively combined.

    Original Sentences

    _____

    _____

    _____

    _____

    Combined Sentence

    _____

    _____

    _____

You may want to use these revised sentences in the final draft of your paragraph.

Part B

Check your paragraph before submitting your final draft.

A CLEAR TOPIC SENTENCE

❏   Does the topic sentence state the topic?

❏   Does the topic sentence state what you will tell about the topic?

CONVINCING SUPPORT

❑ Do your sentences say what you want them to mean?

❑ Have you included enough details to make your ideas clear?

EFFECTIVE ORGANIZATION

❑ Does the paragraph have a beginning, a middle, and an end?

❑ Does your concluding sentence provide a summary of your main idea?

❑ Do you use transitions to link your ideas?

SUCCESSFUL SENTENCES

❑ Is each sentence complete?

❑ Have you eliminated run-ons and fragments?

❑ Have you written each word you need?

❑ Have you used a spell checker, speller, or dictionary to be sure words are spelled correctly?

❑ Have you used the correct form of homonyms?

EFFECTIVE TITLE

❑ Does your title suggest what the paragraph is about and make someone interested in reading it?

Writing from Resources

EXERCISE 12 Share Information

To answers these questions, visit a library or use a search engine on the Internet, such as Lycos, Yahoo, or AltaVista. As you write your answers, use sentence rearrangement and combining techniques.

Your instructor will explain how to complete this section regarding the number of questions to answer and whether to work independently, with a partner, or in a group.

Soup's On

1. What is pop art? Find pictures of some of Andy Warhol's paintings.

2. Why did Andy Warhol paint the tomato soup can?

3. What was the Exposition of 1900? Where was it held? Who attended? What inventions were introduced at this exposition?

4. What is the therapeutic value of chicken soup? How is chicken soup made from scratch?

Sweet, Sticky, Fat-Free Goo

5. What is the marshmallow plant? For what is it used today?

6. How is sugar made? How much sugar is consumed annually by the average American?

7. How is one of the following—fudge, jelly beans, bubble gum, a kind of candy bar, mints—made?

8. Who is Betty Crocker? How has she changed over the years?

9. Who is one cook or chef who has had national prominence? Trace the professional career of this person.

Popcorn

10. What is the history of popcorn?

11. What makes popcorn pop?

12. How was the microwave invented?

13. Why is popcorn a popular snack? What is the nutritional value of popcorn?

14. In addition to popcorn, what are other uses of corn?

Versatile Rice

15. What is the history of growing rice in the United States?

16. Where in the United States is rice grown? How is rice grown?

17. What are the different varieties of rice? What is its nutritional value?

18. What traditions are associated with rice? For example, why is rice thrown at weddings?

19. What is aquaculture? What are the advantages and disadvantages of aquaculture?

Garlic—The Stinking Rose

20. What is the appearance of a garlic plant? What part of the garlic plant is eaten?

21. How is garlic grown? Harvested? Stored?

22. What are some historical beliefs about garlic?

23. What are modern-day beliefs about the benefits of eating garlic?

More About Food

24. What is the food pyramid in the United States? How does it compare with food pyramids from other countries?

25. What are the dangers of eating food that has been improperly handled and stored?

26. What are some safety measures for cooking, handling, and storing food?

27. What is salmonella? How is it spread? What temperatures are the "danger zone"?

28. What is vegetarianism? How can an individual meet nutritional needs without eating meat and dairy products?

EXERCISE 13 Understand Idioms

What is the meaning of each of the following idioms related to food? To find the meaning, check a dictionary or a specialized idiom dictionary, or ask someone who understands the idiom to explain it to you.

baker's dozen

eat one's words

in good taste; in bad taste

be spoon-fed

out of the frying pan and into the fire

land of milk and honey

butterfingers

live on/off the fat of the land

piece of cake

pie in the sky

take with a grain of salt

eat humble pie

born with a silver spoon in one's mouth

CHAPTER 3

Animal Communication

The best thing about animals is that they don't talk much.

— Thornton Wilder (1897–1975)

Do animals "talk" with each other? In this chapter you will read about some animals that seem to interact with one another.

Connecting Reading with Writing

EXERCISE 1   Reflections on Animal Communication

1. What is your definition of intelligence? Give examples.

    _____

    _____

    _____

2. What is your definition of communication? Give examples.

    _____

    _____

    _____

A Perspective on Animal Intelligence

by Marc Washington

1   Animals, from the perspective[1] of some researchers, have been looked down upon because they are considered to be incapable of sophisticated[2] communication and thinking. However, such a belief may only represent our lack of knowledge. In ancient societies, it was assumed that the animal had feelings and thought. In fact, recent research on elephants and killer whales, to mention only several of the animals studied, has revealed extensive communication and maybe even thinking.

2   On October 18, 1997, National Geographic aired a program on NBC Europe featuring the work of the world's most renowned elephantologist, Cynthia Moss, selected by Robert Leaky to head Kenya's Save the Elephant

---

[1] **perspective**   viewpoint, outlook
[2] **sophisticated**   complicated, mature, complex

Program. Moss, who literally[3] lived with elephants in the Anbeselli Sanctuary for over a decade, recorded over 33 elephant vocalizations or *sound concepts* meaning variously, "Let's go. Attack. I'm scared. Don't worry. I'm here." Moss said, "I believe elephants have a range of emotions from joy to grief. And there are even clowns among them. Real clowns."

3   In uniting behind their leader, many social animals *act as one* and through their leader *speak with one voice.* With elephants the matriarch[4] decides when to go into a bog[5] to rescue a young elephant that has fallen in. She decides when to attack a herd of water buffalo contending for the same water hole; when, after crossing a river, to go back to get a youngster crying to them if he is too scared to go into the water; when to lie down and rest in the shade of a grove of trees and when to awaken and go ahead; and when and if to adopt a baby elephant abandoned by another herd as its original mother was too old or sick.

4   Killer whales travel in groupings of families known as pods. Each pod contains upwards of 30 whales that remain together throughout their lives. The pod has its own communication system. The pods use various hunting methods tailor-made for their particular hunting area. NBC Europe aired a National Geographic program on December 27, 1997, documenting the different habits. One pod in Vancouver herds herring. The whales in this pod circle the herring into smaller and smaller circles by swimming around them, keeping in touch with one another through chirps, while driving them to the surface of the water. Once there, they stun large numbers of the herring with a slap of their back fins. One bull male can eat 400 herring a day.

5   At the Cape of Good Hope, near the Antarctic Circle, where there are no herring, only seals and penguins, the whales use a completely different strategy. They plop onto the land and drag seals into the water. The whale's eyesight is good, so when the whales ride on the surface of the water, they can spot baby seals on the beach. It takes the whale parents several years to teach the calves the method of *beaching.* They push the young whales onto the beach and teach them how to rock themselves back into the water. It must require coaxing for a whale parent to convince its bulky child to go onto land. The young are learning a life-threatening ploy. On occasion the 1,000-pound calves do get stuck on the sandy/rocky beaches and die.

[3] **literally**   actually, in reality
[4] **matriarch**   female leader
[5] **bog**   swamp, marsh

6   There is video footage of a killer whale, after having his fill of seals, gently nudging a seal pup perhaps some 100 yards out in the water onto the shore quite unharmed. Just as whale parents gently nudge the baby whales onto the beach to learn how to nab a juicy seal tidbit for lunch, so did the parent whale nudge a seal pup. This time, however, the action was altruistic.

7   How intelligent are animals? In what ways do they communicate? Do they have emotions? These and many other questions provide challenges for researchers. There is a great deal to be learned.

EXERCISE 2   Questions About the Reading

Select the letter that best completes each question or statement.

1. This passage gives evidence that

    A.   ancient people had great love for animals.

    B.   additional research on animal communication is unnecessary.

    C.   animals can teach their offspring.

    D.   animals are intelligent, have feelings, and can think.

2. Choose the sentence that tells the main idea.

    A.   Ancient societies assumed that animals had feelings and thought.

    B.   Recent research on elephants and killer whales, to mention only several of the animals studied, has revealed extensive communication and maybe even thinking.

    C.   In uniting behind their leader, many social animals *act as one* and through their leader *speak with one voice*.

    D.   Animals, from the perspective of some researchers, have been looked down upon because they are considered to be incapable of sophisticated communication and thinking.

3. Before elephants lie down to rest, they

    A.   eat plenty of herring.

    B.   drink from a bog with the water buffalo.

    C.   slide down a riverbank.

    D.   get approval from the head female.

4. Which of the following is most likely true?

    A. The author is an authority on animal intelligence.

    B. The author has an advanced degree in history.

    C. The author supports research on animal communication.

    D. The author has accomplished successful animal research.

5. The author mentions that Cynthia Moss literally lived with elephants in the Anbeselli Sanctuary for over a decade to show that

    A. Moss preferred living with elephants to living with people.

    B. Moss felt safe living with elephants.

    C. Moss had the background to give opinions about elephants.

    D. Moss was fulfilling a childhood dream.

6. As used in the sentence "This time, however, the action was *altruistic*," the word *altruistic* means

    A. unselfish.

    B. cruel.

    C. romantic.

    D. enthusiastic.

EXERCISE 3   Sentence Explication

1. Either use the sentence that follows, or select and copy a different sentence from the reading selection.

    With elephants the matriarch decides when to go into a bog to rescue a young elephant that has fallen in.

    paragraph #3

    Or the sentence you choose:

    _____

    _____

    paragraph #____

2. Paraphrase the sentence by rewriting it in your own words.

_____

_____

_____

_____

3. React to the sentence. What comments and questions do you have about it?

_____

_____

_____

_____

4. Relate to the sentence. What personal experiences does it bring to mind?

_____

_____

_____

_____

_____

_____

_____

EXERCISE 4   Questions for Writing and Discussion

1. What specific information does the author provide to show that both elephants and whales take care of their young?

2. On what evidence does Moss base her belief that elephants have emotions?

3. Why does National Geographic produce programs such as the two described in this reading?

Working from Sentences to Paragraph

Rearrange Sentences with New Beginnings

Live with wolves, and you learn to howl.

— Spanish proverb

EXERCISE 5   Only a Lone Wolf Howls at the Moon

Part A

Use the provided new sentence beginnings to change the emphasis of the following sentences that explain how wolves communicate their feelings and attitudes.

1. The lead wolves in a typical wolf pack of eight to fifteen wolves communicate their power by carrying their tails high and standing tall.

   In a typical wolf pack _____

   _____

   _____

2. To look as fierce as they can during a disagreement, wolves may stick their ears straight up, show their teeth, and bark or growl at each other.

   During a disagreement _____

   _____

   _____

3. The less dominant wolf rolls over on its back to give up rather than fight.

   Giving up _____

   _____

   _____

4. A wolf that is suspicious pulls its ears back and squints.

   A suspicious wolf _____

   _____

   _____

5. A wolf that is fearful flattens its ears against its head.

   A fearful wolf _____

   _____

   _____

6. By dancing around and putting the front of its body down and its back up, a wolf shows that it is ready for play.

   *When a wolf is ready for play*_____

   _____

   _____

7. Wolves howl to find other pack members, to let outside wolves know a territory is taken, or to get the pack ready to hunt.

   By howling _____

   _____

   _____

8. Sometimes it seems as if they howl just for fun.

They sometimes _____

_____

_____

9. Mother wolves make a squeaking noise as they call their pups.

To call their pups _____

_____

_____

10. A system of communication among wolves is needed in their highly social setting.

Wolves _____

_____

_____

Part B

After checking your rearranged sentences with your instructor, copy them to create a paragraph.

Combine Sentences with New Beginnings

Ants are so much like human beings as to be an embarrassment. They farm fungi, raise aphids as livestock, launch armies into war, use chemical sprays to alarm and confuse enemies, capture slaves, engage in child labor, exchange information ceaselessly. They do everything but watch television.

— Lewis Thomas (b. 1913)

EXERCISE 6   Ants in Action

Part A

Read the following draft of a paragraph that explains about insects that live and die for their community. In Parts B and C, you will work on combining sentences and adding transitions to make the paragraph coherent.

There are more than 12,000 different kinds of ants. The ants live throughout the world. In an anthill, there are different kinds of ants. There are queens. There are males. There are workers. Worker ants function in teams. The teams build colonies. They find food. They tend to their young. They remove their dead. The ants communicate with each other. They use chemicals, scent, and touch. Ants can be sociable creatures. They sometimes live as guests with other ants or insects. Ants also have an aggressive nature. Ants fight. Ants feud with other colonies for years. Ants bite. Ants spit out a disagreeable liquid. Ants use their stingers. Some ants run away when under attack. Some ants play dead. Some ants make sound signals to warn others. Ants find their way back to their nest by vision and smell. They orient themselves by the position of the sun. Thousands of ants form a close-knit community. Thousands of ants inhabit a single anthill.

Part B

Combine the ideas from the sentences in each group to write one new sentence. Begin the new sentence using the indicated words. As you write the sentence, think about the emphasis and relationships you want to achieve.

1.

There are more than 12,000 different kinds of ants.

The ants live throughout the world.

Living _____

_____

_____

2.

In an anthill, there are different kinds of ants.

There are queens.

There are males.

There are workers.

Queens _____

_____

_____

3.

Worker ants function in teams.

The teams build colonies.

They find food.

They tend to their young.

They remove their dead.

Functioning in teams _____

_____

_____

4.

The ants communicate with each other.

They use chemicals, scent, and touch.

To communicate _____

_____

_____

5.

Ants can be sociable creatures.

They sometimes live as guests with other ants or insects.

Since _____

_____

_____

6.

Ants also have an aggressive nature.

Ants can feud with other colonies for years.

With _____

_____

_____

7.

Ants fight.

Ants bite.

Ants spit out a disagreeable liquid.

Ants use their stingers.

Ants fight by _____

_____

_____

8.

Some ants run away when under attack.

Some ants play dead.

Some ants make sound signals to warn others.

When _____

_____

_____

9.

Ants find their way back to their nest by vision and smell.

They orient themselves by the position of the sun.

To find _____

_____

_____

10.

Thousands of ants form a close-knit community.

Thousands of ants inhabit a single anthill.

In a single anthill _____

_____

_____

Part C

After checking your combined sentences with your instructor, copy them to create a paragraph. Add transitions and linking words to make the paragraph coherent. Note the differences between the original and the rewritten paragraphs.

Combine Sentences on Your Own

*The voice of the wild goose caught by the bait
cries out.*

— *Love Songs of the New Kingdom*
(1550–1080 B.C.)

EXERCISE 7   In V-Formation

Part A

Read the following draft of an informative paragraph about community behavior among Canadian geese. In Parts B and C, you will work on combining sentences and adding transitions to make the paragraph coherent.

Migrating geese are often seen flying. They fly in V-formation. Flying in V-formation creates updrafts of air. The birds use less energy to fly. A lead goose gets tired. Another goose takes the lead. The geese honk to each other as they fly. The geese appear to encourage each other. Sometimes a goose gets sick or wounded. Two other geese drop out of formation. These two geese follow to help and protect it. They stay with the goose in trouble. The goose dies or is able to fly again. The geese may catch up with the flock. The geese may fly with another formation. Geese have reasons to fly in formation. They are able to fly farther. They are able to communicate with each other.

Part B

Revise the paragraph by combining the ideas from the sentences in each group to write one new sentence. As you write each sentence, think about the emphasis and relationships you want to achieve, adding transition and linking words as needed.

1.

Migrating geese are often seen flying.

They fly in V-formation.

_____

_____

_____

_____

2.

Flying in V-formation creates updrafts of air.

The birds use less energy to fly.

_____

_____

_____

_____

3.

A lead goose gets tired.

Another goose takes the lead.

_____

_____

_____

_____

4.

The geese honk to each other as they fly.

The geese appear to encourage each other.

_____

_____

_____

_____

5.

Sometimes a goose gets sick or wounded.

Two other geese drop out of formation.

These two geese follow to help and protect it.

_____

_____

_____

_____

6.

They stay with the goose in trouble.

The goose dies or is able to fly again.

_____

_____

_____

_____

7.

The geese may catch up with the flock.

The geese may fly with another formation.

_____

_____

_____

_____

8.

Geese have reasons to fly in formation.

They are able to fly farther.

They are able to communicate with each other.

_____

_____

_____

_____

Part C

After you have checked your sentences with your instructor, copy them to create a coherent paragraph. Note the differences between the original and the rewritten paragraphs.

Identify Sentences in Context

*When you go in search of honey, you must
expect to be stung by bees.*

— Kenneth Kaunda (b. 1924)

EXERCISE 8   The Dance of the Honeybee

**The following paragraph about the communication of honeybees is missing
periods. Add a period to mark the end of a sentence and capitalize the beginning word of the next sentence. Copy on the adjacent numbered line each
word you have capitalized.**

Honeybees use a sophisticated form of communica-	1. _____
tion called the waggle dance to let other bees know	2. _____
about a new supply of pollen or nectar when a bee	3. _____
discovers a new source of food, such as a field of	4. _____
fresh clover, she fills her honey sac with nectar and	5. _____
returns to the hive there she performs a vigorous, but	6. _____
highly standardized dance, to show the others the	7. _____
direction and the distance to the food if the source is	8. _____
within 100 yards of the hive, the bee performs a cir-	9. _____
cular dance, first moving about an inch and then cir-	10. _____
cling in the opposite direction the speed of the dance	11. _____
and its length can communicate the relative ease or	12. _____
difficulty of the flight uphill flights or flights against	13. _____
the wind take more energy if the amount of food is	14. _____
great, the dance lasts longer and is more enthusiastic	15. _____
numerous bees in the hive closely follow the dancer,	16. _____
imitating her movements during this ceremony the	17. _____
other workers smell the fragrance of the flowers from	18. _____

which the dancer collected the nectar having learned

that food is not far from the hive and what it smells

like, other bees leave the hive and fly in widening cir-

cles until they find the source by relating information

about the location and amount of food, honeybees

may be superior to all other animals, except humans,

in their ability to communicate complex ideas.

19. _____

20. _____

21. _____

22. _____

23. _____

24. _____

25. _____

Rearrange and Combine Sentences Using Transitions

> Man [has] always assumed that he was more
> intelligent than dolphins because he had
> achieved so much—the wheel, New York, wars
> and so on—while all the dolphins had ever
> done was muck about in the water having a
> good time. But conversely, the dolphins have
> always believed that they were far more
> intelligent than man—for precisely
> the same reason.
>
> — Douglas Noel Adams (b. 1952)

EXERCISE 9   Dolphins

Part A

Read a draft of an informative paragraph about an intelligent mammal. In Parts B and C, you will work on combining, rearranging, and adding transitions to make the paragraph coherent.

Humans seem to have an equivalent in the ocean. The equivalent in the ocean is the dolphin. Dolphins have a system of communication. They click. They whistle. They whine. They groan. They clap their jaws together loudly. Dolphins communicate when they are feeding. They communicate when they are in distress. They communicate when they are happy. They also use body language. They jump out of the water and fall back into it with a loud splash. They slap the water surface. Dolphins communicate in a sophisticated way. Scientists want to learn more.

Part B

Revise the paragraph by using rearrangement, combining, and transitions *wherever appropriate* to create new sentences. Not every sentence needs to be rewritten.

1. Humans seem to have an equivalent in the ocean.

2. The equivalent in the ocean is the dolphin.

3. Dolphins have a system of communication.

4. They click.

5. They whistle.

6. They whine.

7. They groan.

8. They clap their jaws together loudly.

9. Dolphins communicate when they are feeding.

10. They communicate when they are in distress.

11. They communicate when they are happy.

12. They also use body language.

13. They jump out of the water and fall back into it with a loud splash.

14. They slap the water surface.

15. Dolphins communicate in a sophisticated way.

16. Scientists want to learn more.

Part C

After you have checked your sentences with your instructor, copy them to create a paragraph. Note the differences between the original and the rewritten paragraphs.

Writing from Experience

EXERCISE 10   Write a Paragraph

Write a paragraph of 8–12 sentences on one of the following topics.

1.   Technology provides effective ways for people to communicate over time and over distance. In addition to face-to-face communication, how do you communicate? Tell about one way you communicate with people who are not in the same place that you are.

     Questions to Consider

     What is your method of communication?

     With whom do you communicate?

     How often do you communicate? How much time do you spend?

     What are the advantages or disadvantages of this method of communication?

2.   Like packs of wolves, when groups of people gather there generally are dominant and more submissive individuals. Tell how an individual you know dominates a group.

     Questions to Consider

     What is the group? How many are in the group?

     Who is the dominant member of the group? How do you know? (consider appearance, behavior, and conversation)

     What are the reactions of other people in the group?

     Do you believe this person will continue to dominate?

3. Just as ants work together in a community, humans also work together to meet their needs. Tell about your involvement in a community, whether it is in your family, neighborhood, school, or place of employment.

    Questions to Consider

    What is your role in your community?

    Why do you have this role?

    What do you do in this role?

    How is what you do helpful to your community?

    Is this role ongoing, or do you envision it changing over time? Explain.

4. Communicating with an animal takes special skills, especially when you are attempting to teach the animal to perform a task. Tell about a time that you trained a pet or other animal to do something.

    Questions to Consider

    What kind of animal were you working with?

    What did you teach the animal to do?

    What were your techniques for teaching the animal?

    How did the animal react?

    Were you pleased with your efforts?

For question 5, you are on your own to write your own questions for development.

5. Animals and humans appear to share the capacity to care for others who need help. Tell about how you helped another individual with physical or emotional needs or how someone helped you.

    Questions for Development

    _____

    _____

    _____

    _____

    _____

For question 6, you are on your own to create a focus as well as your own questions for development.

6. Write on a topic related to animal communication or intelligence.

    Focus

    _____

    Questions for Development

    _____

    _____

    _____

    _____

    _____

EXERCISE 11   Revise Your Paragraph

Part A

Reread the paragraph you wrote for Exercise 10.

1. Choose one sentence to rearrange.

    Original Sentence _____

    _____

    Rearranged Sentence _____

    _____

2. Choose two or more sentences that could be effectively combined.

    Original Sentence

    _____

    _____

_____

_____

Combined Sentences

_____

_____

_____

You may want to use these revised sentences in the final draft of your paragraph.

Part B
Check your paragraph before submitting your final draft.

A CLEAR TOPIC SENTENCE

❐ Does the topic sentence state the topic?

❐ Does the topic sentence state what you will tell about the topic?

CONVINCING SUPPORT

❐ Do your sentences say what you want them to mean?

❐ Have you included enough details to make your ideas clear?

EFFECTIVE ORGANIZATION

❐ Does the paragraph have a beginning, a middle, and an end?

❐ Does your concluding sentence provide a summary of your main idea?

❐ Do you use transitions to link your ideas?

SUCCESSFUL SENTENCES

❐ Is each sentence complete?

❐ Have you eliminated run-ons and fragments?

❐ Have you written each word you need?

❐ Have you used a spell checker, speller, or dictionary to be sure words are spelled correctly?

❐ Have you used the correct form of homonyms?

EFFECTIVE TITLE

❑ Does your title suggest what the paragraph is about? Does the title make someone want to read the paragraph?

Writing from Resources

EXERCISE 12 Share Information

To answer these questions, visit a library or use a search engine on the Internet, such as Lycos, Yahoo, or AltaVista. As you write your answers, use sentence rearrangement and combining techniques.

Your instructor will explain how to complete this section regarding the number of questions to answer and whether to work independently, with a partner, or in a group.

Only a Lone Wolf Howls at the Moon

1. What are the physical characteristics of a wolf?

2. What is a wolf pack?

3. Which wolves in the pack reproduce? What is the gestation period? Who cares for the baby wolves? What are some interesting facts about their development?

4. After being near extinction, how are wolves being reintroduced in the United States? How is telemetry used to track wolves? What are the problems? What are the successes?

Ants in Action

5. What makes ant jaws extremely powerful? Why are the antennae important?

6. What are anteaters? What is unique about their eating habits?

7. What problems are caused by army ants? Carpenter ants?

8. What is amber? What do scientists learn from studying it?

In V-Formation

9. What are the distinguishing characteristics of Canadian geese?

10. What is the annual migration pattern of Canadian geese?

11. What are the characteristics of the family life of Canadian geese?

12. What are the conflicts between people and geese?

The Dance of the Honeybee

13. What are the various castes of honeybees inside a hive? What is the job of each group?

14. What is honeycomb? Describe it and its function.

15. What are killer bees? Why are they a concern to beekeepers in the United States?

16. What is apitherapy?

17. How can people avoid bee stings? What is effective treatment for stings?

Dolphins

18. What is the anatomy of the dolphin—exterior, interior, and skeletal?

19. How does a dolphin swim? What is the dolphin's fastest swimming speed? How is the dolphin's skin an aid in swimming?

20. What is the dolphin's relationship with humans? How do humans threaten the dolphin population?

21. How do dolphins communicate using sound? Echolocation? Other techniques?

More About Animal Communication

22. How do chimpanzees communicate with each other? With humans?

23. What is involved in teaching a bird to talk? Does the bird understand what it says?

EXERCISE 13   Understand Idioms

What is the meaning of each of the following idioms related to animals? To find the meaning, check a dictionary, or a specialized idiom dictionary, or ask someone who understands the idiom to explain it to you.

cry wolf

whale of a job

wild goose chase

kill the goose that lays the golden egg

big fish in a small pond

fish for information

Mother Goose

wolf in sheep's clothing

silly goose

goose egg

bee in one's bonnet

make a bee line

flea market

dog days

quilting bee

spelling bee

talk about the birds and the bees

something is for the birds

talking turkey

dog-eat-dog world

monkey business

white elephant

CHAPTER 4

Weather

Everybody talks about the weather, but nobody does anything about it.

— attributed to Mark Twain
(1835–1910)

For many people, weather is so important they use climate as a factor in deciding where they want to live. Weather can have a profound effect on people's health, as explained in the reading for this chapter.

Connecting Reading with Writing

EXERCISE 1   Reflections on Weather

1. What is your source of information about the day's weather? Is the information generally accurate?

    _____

    _____

    _____

2. Would you consider moving to an area with a different climate? Why or why not?

    _____

    _____

    _____

Changeable as the Weather

by Dianne J. Moore

1   A few years ago my sister and I vacationed in St. Louis to celebrate the twenty-fifth anniversary of the city's famous Gateway Arch. I was looking forward to enjoying time with my sister and just having some fun at the festivities; that is, until the weather changed my plans. The temperatures in St. Louis—which had exceeded 90 degrees for days on end before our arrival—plunged into the 60s while rain drenched the city for the entire four days we were there. Much to my chagrin,[1] I was incapacitated with

---

[1] **chagrin**   unease, regret

agonizing arthritic back pain during the entire vacation, and my sister had to attend many of the festivities alone.

2 According to Stephen Rosen, M.D., author of *Weathering: How the Atmosphere Conditions Your Body, Your Mind, Your Moods—and Your Health,* healthy people are often affected by no fewer than 37 symptoms during changes in temperature, humidity, wind, and sunlight. The most frequent complaint is tiredness, followed by bad moods, disinterest in work, head pressure, insomnia, and headaches.

3 In his unique study several years ago, Joseph Hollander, M.D., professor emeritus of medicine at the University of Pennsylvania, constructed a special room, called a climatron, where he controlled weather conditions. Whenever conditions in the climatron simulated a thunderstorm, falling air pressure, and rising humidity, arthritis symptoms worsened in all but one of his 12 subjects. A steady, warm, and dry environment did not aggravate arthritis symptoms in these people.

4 Recently, Dr. Robert N. Jamison and colleagues at Brigham and Women's Hospital in Boston surveyed 558 chronic[2] pain patients—those with backache, headache, arthritis, and the like—in four cities nationwide and found that weather affects pain no matter where you live. "The real culprit," explains Jamison, "may be a change in barometric pressure, since patients are most likely to report an increase in pain in advance of weather conditions."

5 When the outside pressure falls, tendons, ligaments, muscles, and bones swell and readjust, pressing on sensitized nerves throughout the body. Headaches, particularly migraines, become severe when there is a drop in barometric pressure, and surgical scar tissue, which differs from original cells, is more sensitive when the weather is wet and stormy. In the summertime, high winds can fill the air with ragweed and various pollutants, leaving those who suffer from allergies or asthma gasping for breath.

6 People generally feel most comfortable when the temperature is about 70 and the humidity about 50 percent. Whenever the temperature changes significantly, your body struggles to regulate its internal temperature against the outside elements. If your body temperature climbs to 105 degrees or higher during a heat wave, brain damage can follow within minutes. Body temperature that dips below 95 degrees in response to extreme cold weather is clearly dangerous; by some estimates no less than 35,000 deaths occur each year from cold stress. In addition, colder weather thickens the albumin-like fluid around the joints and tendons, allowing less movement.

[2] **chronic**   lasting a long time

7   Day-to-day and season-to-season weather changes not only affect physical health but also take a toll on behavior and moods. No one knows this better than Barb Baird, 45, a volunteer with the Michigan Salvation Army. During autumn the falling and molding of the leaves aggravate her allergies and weaken her immune system. "With the continued lack of rest comes orneriness," she says. "When I don't feel well, I lose my ability to care about others." Even worse, dry, warm winds, such as the foehn in Switzerland, the sharav in Israel, and the Santa Anas in California, have been associated with an increase in crime, murder, and assaultive behavior.

8   During the fall and winter months, Neal Owens, of Gaithersburg, Maryland, watched his marriage collapse and almost lost his job because of depression. He volunteered for a medical study into seasonal affective disorder (SAD)—a mood disorder precipitated by decreased sunlight between October and April.

9   "This depression occurs at a particular time of year on a repeated basis," explains Paul Goodnick, Ph.D., director of the Mood Disorders Program at the University of Miami in Florida. "What distinguishes it from other forms of depression is that it fades almost spontaneously during the springtime."

10   The good news is that 75 percent of people affected by SAD find relief with the use of a medical light box that transmits a full-spectrum fluorescent light equivalent to midday natural light. The body doesn't know the difference between natural sunlight and the medical light boxes; both help the body to release two depression-fighting chemicals—melatonin and serotonin. With the improved light boxes in use today, patients get relief sitting in front of the light box from 15 minutes to two hours per day.

11   "But if you stop using the box," warns Goodnick, "you go right back to where you were before the light therapy." If you think you might be affected by SAD, discuss it with your doctor.

12   Ironically, the arrival of spring and sunshine is not an uplifting experience for everyone. Statistics show that suicides peak during March and April. The arrival of spring brings the spirit of renewal for all but depressed people, who feel anything but springlike inside. The newness all around them only makes their "winter of discontent" all the more obvious to them. All this doesn't mean that, if you're weather-sensitive, you're doomed to a life of fluctuating pain, bad health, and mood swings.

13   The most important thing, say the experts, is to remember that although you can't control the weather, you can control your responses to it. "So on those inescapable, cloudy, gloomy, damp days," says meterologist Joel Sobel, of Accu-Weather, Inc., in State College, Pennsylvania, "try to keep an optimistic attitude and get through it, as opposed to letting life wash over you. Like Little Orphan Annie said, 'The sun will come out tomorrow.'"

EXERCISE 2   Questions About the Reading

Select the letter that best completes each question or statement.

1. The passage focuses mainly on

    A. predicting the weather.

    B. doing someting about the weather.

    C. feeling the effects of the weather.

    D. controlling the weather.

2. Choose the sentence that tells the main idea.

    A. Healthy people are often affected by no fewer than 37 symptoms during changes in temperature, humidity, wind, and sunlight.

    B. The most important thing, say the experts, is to remember that although you can't control the weather, you can control your responses to it.

    C. Day-to-day and season-to-season weather changes not only affect physical health but also take a toll on behavior and moods.

    D. Ironically, the arrival of spring and sunshine is not an uplifting experience for everyone.

3. Which of the following is not mentioned in this passage as a weather condition that has an effect on people?

    A. snow

    B. cold

    C. humidity

    D. sun

4. Which of the following is most likely true?

    A. The author's sister is unaffected by changes in weather.

    B. The author is a trained meteorologist.

    C. The author feels better when the weather is warm and dry.

    D. The author knows little about the effect of weather on humans.

5. The author mentions the climatron as evidence that Dr. Hollander

    A. does everything he can to heal his patients.

    B. does not enjoy being outdoors in the rain.

    C. is conducting research on a cure for arthritis.

    D. is studying how weather affects arthritis.

6. As used in the sentence, "During autumn the falling and molding of the leaves *aggravate* her allergies and weaken her immune system," the word *aggravate* means

    A. soothe.

    B. worsen.

    C. anger.

    D. control.

EXERCISE 3 Sentence Explication

1. Either use the sentence that follows, or select and copy a different sentence from the reading selection.

> *The most important thing, say the experts, is to remember that although you can't control the weather, you can control your responses to it.*

paragraph #12

Or the sentence you choose:

_____

_____

paragraph #____

2. Paraphrase the sentence by rewriting it in your own words.

_____

_____

_____

_____

3. React to the sentence. What comments and questions do you have about it?

_____

_____

_____

_____

_____

4. Relate to the sentence. What personal experiences does it bring to mind?

_____

_____

_____

_____

_____

_____

_____

EXERCISE 4   Questions for Writing and Discussion

1. What is a climatron? What is its value?

2. In what weather do people generally feel most comfortable?

3. What is seasonal affective disorder (SAD)? How is this disorder treated?

4. What is the meaning of Little Orphan Annie's words, "The sun will come out tomorrow"?

Working from Sentences to Paragraph

Rearrange Sentences with New Beginnings

A proverb is a short sentence based on long experience.

— Miguel de Cervantes (1547–1616)

EXERCISE 5   Weather Lore

Part A

Use the provided new sentence beginnings to change the emphasis of the following sentences that explain what old-time sayings tell about the weather. As you rearrange the words, be sure to keep the meaning of the original sentence.

1.   For thousands of years, observations about the weather were made by people.

For thousands of years, people _____

_____

_____

2.   Some of these observations have resulted in easy-to-remember sayings or proverbs.

Easy-to-remember sayings _____

_____

_____

3. Do you think any of these proverbs are true?

   Which _____

   _____

   _____

4. It will rain when leaves show their backs.

   When leaves _____

   _____

   _____

5. On a wooly bear caterpillar, the wider the middle band, the milder the climate.

   The wider the middle band _____

   _____

   _____

6. There will be a snowfall in winter for every fog in August.

   For every fog in August _____

   _____

   _____

7. Get a fair warning from a rainbow in the morning.

   A rainbow in the morning _____

   _____

   _____

8. Rainy weather is at stake when your joints all start to ache.

   When your joints _____

   _____

   _____

9. Farmers and mariners, who were especially concerned with the weather, attempted forecasts based on weather lore and personal observations.

   Because _____

   _____

   _____

Part B

After checking your rearranged sentences with your instructor, copy them to create a paragraph.

Combine Sentences with New Beginnings

Nature does nothing uselessly.

— Aristotle (348–322 B.C.)

EXERCISE 6   Meteorology

Part A

Read the following draft of an informative paragraph about how people predict the weather. In Parts B and C, you will work on combining sentences and adding transitions to make the paragraph coherent.

A weather forecast is the result of worldwide effort. This effort is made by thousands of meteorologists. The meteorologists work in national weather services in many countries. Weather observers record atmospheric measurements around the world. There are more than 10,000 surface weather stations. There are over 7,000 ships and oil rigs at sea. First, the data is transmitted to regional and national centers in the United States. Next, the data is transmitted to three World Meteorological Organization Centers (WMO). Meteorologists at the WMO centers assemble the data. They create weather maps. They enter the data into computer programs. They produce global forecasts. This happens about every six hours. The maps are distirbuted to national weather services. The forecasts are distributed to national weather services. In the United States, NOAA is responsible for supplying information about the weather. NOAA is an abbreviation for the National Oceanic and Atmospheric Administration. NOAA provides current conditions and weather warnings. NOAA prepares weather maps, storm predictions, and extended forecasts.

Part B

Combine the ideas from the sentences in each group to write one new sentence. Begin the new sentence using the indicated words. As you write the sentence, think about the emphasis and relationships you want to achieve.

1.

A weather forecast is the result of worldwide effort.

This effort is made by thousands of meteorologists.

The meteorologists work in national weather services in many countries.

A weather forecast _____

_____

_____

_____

2.

Weather observers record atmospheric measurements around the world.

There are more than 10,000 surface weather stations.

There are over 7,000 ships and oil rigs at sea.

Around the world _____

_____

_____

_____

3.

First, the data is transmitted to regional and national centers in the United States.

Next, the data is transmitted to three World Meteorological Organization Centers (WMO).

After the data _____

_____

_____

_____

4.

Meteorologists at the WMO centers assemble the data.

They create weather maps.

They enter the data into computer programs.

They produce global forecasts.

Assembling _____

_____

_____

_____

5.

This happens about every six hours.

The maps are distributed to national weather services.

The forecasts are distributed to national weather services.

About every six hours _____

_____

_____

_____

6.

In the United States, NOAA is responsible for supplying information about the weather.

NOAA is an abbreviation for the National Oceanic and Atmospheric Administration.

The National Oceanic and Atmospheric Administration _____

_____

_____

_____

7.

NOAA provides current conditions and weather warnings.

NOAA prepares weather maps, storm predictions, and extended forecasts.

In addition to _____

_____

_____

_____

Part C

After checking your combined sentences with your instructor, copy them to create a paragraph. Add transitions and linking words to make the paragraph coherent. Note the differences between the original and the rewritten paragraphs.

Combine Sentences on Your Own

The greater difficulty, the more glory there is in surrounding it. Skillful pilots gain their reputation from storms and tempests.

— Epicurus (341–270 B.C.)

EXERCISE 7   Hurricanes

Part A

Read the following draft of a descriptive paragraph about the immense power of hurricanes. In Parts B and C, you will work on combining sentences and adding transitions to make the paragraph coherent.

Hurricanes have an immense destructive force. Hurricanes can last for weeks. Hurricanes can cover thousands of miles. A full-fledged hurricane can produce sustained winds of 150 miles per hour. With gusts, the hurricane can reach winds of up to 190 miles per hour. A hurricane may contain hundreds of thunderstorms. A hurricane may measure up to 600 miles in diameter. The hurricane has two main parts. There is the eye of the hurricane. There is the wall of clouds. The eye of the hurricane is the calm area. It is in the center of the storm. It measures about 20 miles in diameter. The second part is the wall of clouds. It surrounds the calm. That is where the strongest winds and heaviest rains occur. A hurricane begins in warm tropical oceans. Heat, moisture, and wind fuel the hurricane. Winds grow around the eye of the hurricane. The winds have great velocity. The winds have ferocious energy. The winds produce enormous waves. The enormous waves move ashore. The enormous waves flood large areas of coastal land. The enormous waves cause widespread damage. About five hurricanes strike the United States coastline every three years. Of these five, two will be major hurricanes.

Part B

Revise the paragraph by combining the ideas from the sentences in each group to write one new sentence. As you write each sentence, think about the emphasis and relationships you want to achieve, adding transitions and linking words as needed.

1.

Hurricanes have an immense destructive force.

Hurricanes can last for weeks.

Hurricanes can cover thousands of miles.

_____

_____

_____

2.

A full-fledged hurricane can produce sustained winds of 150 miles per hour.

With gusts, the hurricane can reach winds of up to 190 miles per hour.

_____

_____

_____

3.

A hurricane may contain hundreds of thunderstorms.

A hurricane may measure up to 600 miles in diameter.

_____

_____

_____

4.

The hurricane has two main parts.

There is the eye of the hurricane.

There is the wall of clouds.

_____

_____

_____

_____

5.

The eye of the hurricane is the calm area.

It is in the center of the storm.

It measures about 20 miles in diameter.

_____

_____

_____

_____

6.

The second part is the wall of clouds.

It surrounds the calm.

That is where the strongest winds and heaviest rains occur.

_____

_____

_____

_____

7.

A hurricane begins in warm tropical oceans.

Heat, moisture, and wind fuel the hurricane.

_____

_____

_____

_____

8.

Winds grow around the eye of the hurricane.

The winds have great velocity.

The winds have ferocious energy.

The winds produce enormous waves.

_____

_____

_____

_____

9.

The enormous waves move ashore.

The enormous waves flood large areas of coastal land.

The enormous waves cause widespread damage.

_____

_____

_____

_____

10.

About five hurricanes strike the United States coastline every three years.

Of these five, two will be major hurricanes.

_____

_____

_____

_____

Part C

After you have checked your sentences with your instructor, copy them to create a coherent paragraph. Note the differences between the original and the rewritten paragraphs.

Identifying Sentences in Context

_____

Words like winter snowflakes . . .

— Homer (c. 700 B.C.)

_____

EXERCISE 8   Snowflakes

The following paragraph about ice crystals is missing periods. Add a period to mark the end of a sentence and capitalize the beginning word of the next sentence. Copy on the adjacent numbered line each word you have capitalized.

High in a cold sky, crystals of all shapes and sizes	1. _____
begin as molecules of water vapor and freeze around	2. _____
tiny particles as the ice crystals cling to each other,	3. _____
they form snowflakes once the snowflakes are heavy	4. _____

enough, they fall to the ground when hundreds of
individual crystals join together, they can produce a
snowflake as large as three to four inches in diameter
the saying that no two snowflakes are identical is correct because the infinite variability of weather conditions makes each snow crystal unique although all ice
crystals are hexagonal and symmetrical, the arrange-
ment of the water molecules in the snow crystal can
be shaped as thin plates, needles, hollow columns,
sector plates, or dendrites the large number of reflect-
ing surfaces of the crystal makes snow appear white
to date, the heaviest snowfall within 24 hours was 76
inches at Silver Lake, Colorado, on April 15, 1921.

5. _____
6. _____
7. _____
8. _____
9. _____
10. _____
11. _____
12. _____
13. _____
14. _____
15. _____
16. _____
17. _____

Rearrange and Combine Sentences Using Transitions

*The wind goeth toward the south and turneth
about unto the north; it whirleth about
continually, and the wind returneth again
according to his circuits.*

— Ecclesiastes 1:6

EXERCISE 9   Tornadoes

Part A

Read a draft of a paragraph describing the terrifying force of tornadoes. In Parts B and C, you will work on combining, rearranging, and adding transitions to make the paragraph coherent.

A tornado is a violently spinning whirlpool of air. A tornado extends from the base of a storm cloud to the ground. It is associated with severe storm activity. It is one of nature's most destructive phenomena. A tornado is capable of generating winds up to 300 miles per hour. The United States is by far the most tornado-prone country in the world. There are about 750 tornadoes annually. Most tornadoes occur in the Great Plains. Oklahoma experiences more tornadoes per acre than any other location on earth. A tornado's movement is often erratic.[1] For instance, a tornado may destroy one house when houses on either side of it are untouched. Tornadoes can occur in isolation. Tornadoes can occur together in great numbers. Tornadoes can last for minutes or hours. Tornadoes can strike at a single location or travel from location to location for several hundred miles.

Part B

Revise the paragraph by using rearrangement, combining, and transitions *wherever appropriate* to create new sentences. Not every sentence needs to be rewritten.

1. A tornado is a violently spinning whirlpool of air.

2. A tornado extends from the base of a storm cloud to the ground.

3. It is associated with severe storm activity.

4. It is one of nature's most destructive phenomena.

5. A tornado is capable of generating winds up to 300 miles per hour.

6. The United States is by far the most tornado-prone country in the world.

7. There are about 750 tornadoes annually.

8. Most tornadoes occur in the Great Plains.

9. Oklahoma experiences more tornadoes per acre than any other location on earth.

10. A tornado's movement is often erratic.

11. For instance, a tornado may destroy one house when houses on either side of it are untouched.

---

[1] **erratic**   having no certain course; wandering; uncertain

12. Tornadoes can occur in isolation.

13. Tornadoes can occur together in great numbers.

14. Tornadoes can last for minutes or hours.

15. Tornadoes can strike at a single location or travel from location to location for several hundred miles.

Part C

After you have checked your sentences with your instructor, copy them to create a paragraph. Note the differences between the original and the rewritten paragraphs.

Writing from Experience

EXERCISE 10   Write a Paragraph

Write a paragraph of 8–12 sentences on one of the following topics.

1. Some people can't wait for the snowy days of winter. Others long for the heat and humidity of a hot August afternoon. There are those who look forward to waking up to enjoy a rainy day while others love the sunshine. Write about your favorite type of weather.

   Questions to Consider

   What weather do you prefer?

   What activities do you do?

   How does the weather make you feel physically? Emotionally?

2. Some people's most powerful memories come from having lived through a storm. During bad weather, everyday life is interrupted. Supplies may be unavailable, property may be affected, and there may even be personal tragedy. Write about a time when you experienced severe weather.

Questions to Consider

What was the weather condition?

How old were you?

Where were you living?

What happened during the severe weather?

How did the weather impact you?

3. In an ideal world, perhaps an order could be given to the meteorologists about the kind of weather needed for a particular day. In reality, no matter what the plans, the weather is whatever it is. Write about a time when the weather was what you had hoped for or a time when the weather did not cooperate with your plans.

Questions to Consider

What was the occasion? What weather were you hoping for?

What was the weather like for the occasion?

How did the weather enhance the occasion? Or, how did it interfere with the occasion?

If you had known what the weather was going to be, how would you have changed your plans?

4. The meteorological conditions in a particular area are called "climate." You may be satisfied with the climate in which you are living, or you may find it has limitations. Write an evaluation of your area's climate.

Questions to Consider

Are you satisfied with the climate where you live?

What are characteristics of this climate?

What makes the climate appealing or unappealing for you?

Do you intend to remain living where you do? Why or why not?

For question 5, you are on your own to create questions for development.

5. Many people find "saving for a rainy day" an important part of life. What is saved may be money, time, energy, or something else. Tell about a time "saving for a rainy day" worked or did not work for you.

    Questions for Development

    _____

    _____

    _____

    _____

For question 6, you are on your own to decide a focus and to create questions for development.

6. Write on a topic of your choice about weather.

    Focus

    _____

    Questions for Development

    _____

    _____

    _____

    _____

    _____

EXERCISE 11   Revise Your Paragraph

Part A
Reread the paragraph you wrote for Exercise 10.

1. Choose one sentence to rearrange.

   Original Sentence _____

   _____

   Rearranged Sentence _____

   _____

2. Choose two or more sentences that could be effectively combined.

   Original Sentences

   _____

   _____

   _____

   Combined Sentence

   _____

   _____

   You may want to use these revised sentences in the final draft of your paragraph.

Part B
Check your paragraph before submitting your final draft.

A CLEAR TOPIC SENTENCE
❐   Does the topic sentence state the topic?

❐   Does the topic sentence state what you will tell about the topic?

CONVINCING SUPPORT
❐   Do your sentences say what you want them to mean?

❐   Have you included enough details to make your ideas clear?

EFFECTIVE ORGANIZATION

❏ Does the paragraph have a beginning, a middle, and an end?

❏ Does your concluding sentence provide a summary of your main idea?

❏ Do you use transitions to link your ideas?

SUCCESSFUL SENTENCES

❏ Is each sentence complete?

❏ Have you eliminated run-ons and fragments?

❏ Have you written each word you need?

❏ Have you used a spell checker, speller, or dictionary to be sure words are spelled correctly?

❏ Have you used the correct form of homonyms?

EFFECTIVE TITLE

❏ Does your title suggest what the paragraph is about and make someone interested in reading it?

Writing from Resources

EXERCISE 12   Share Information

To answer these questions, visit a library or use a search engine on the Internet, such as Lycos, Yahoo, or AltaVista.

Your instructor will explain how to complete this section regarding the number of questions to answer and whether to work independently, with a partner, or in a group.

Weather Lore

1. Locate and describe world climate zones. A diagram may be useful.

2. What is the origin of the *Old Farmer's Almanac?* What information does the almanac provide today?

3. What is the legend of Groundhog Day?

Meteorology

4. Who was Aristotle? What were his contributions to meteorology?

5. Who was Benjamin Franklin? What were his contributions to meteorology?

6. What is relative humidity? How does it affect people?

7. What is the wind chill factor? Use a chart to explain.

8. What is the heat index factor? Use a chart to explain.

Hurricanes

9. What is the difference between a tropical storm and a hurricane? What system does the National Hurricane Service use for naming hurricanes?

10. What should a person do during a hurricane?

Snowflakes

11. Who was Wilson A. "Snowflake" Bentley? For what reasons was he well-known?

12. What is a blizzard? What is hail?

13. What do the following terms mean: winter storm outlook, winter storm watch, blizzard warning, winter storm warning, wind chill warning.

14. What should individuals do if they are in a car during a winter storm or blizzard?

Tornadoes

15. What is the difference between a tornado watch and a tornado warning? What are tornado danger signs?

16. What should individuals do during a tornado if they are at home? At work or school? Outdoors? In a car?

17. How are tornadoes forecast today?

More About Weather

18. How do El Niño and La Niña impact the weather in the United States?

19. What are the safety guidelines for individuals caught near lightning? What is the 30/30 lightning rule?

20. What safety guidelines should individuals know about very hot weather in terms of food intake, attire, being outdoors, traveling?

21. What safety guidelines should individuals know about very cold weather in terms of food intake, attire, being outdoors, traveling?

EXERCISE 13   Understand Idioms

What is the meaning of each of the following idioms related to weather? To find the meaning, check a dictionary or a specialized idiom dictionary, or ask someone who understands the idiom to explain it to you.

fair-weather friend

weather the storm

be under the weather

be snowed under

in the eye of the storm

whistle in the wind

calm before the storm

ride out the storm

tempest in a teapot

steal one's thunder

rain cats and dogs

be under a cloud

have one's head in the clouds

on cloud nine

CHAPTER 5

Civility

Make everything you do your religion, and
everything you say your prayer.

— Anonymous

Being a member of a group involves accepting a code of behavior. The reading in this chapter is about a suggested standard of behavior for civilized people.

Connecting Reading with Writing

EXERCISE 1   Reflections on Civility

1. What is civility? Why is civility a necessity for people living in "civilization"?

   _____

   _____

   _____

2. Is there a difference between civility and good manners? Explain.

   _____

   _____

   _____

Americans for More Civility

by Pam Easton

1   It's a lesson every mother teaches. But as the pace of life quickens, a Texas man and his Georgia friend say people are quickly forgetting the civility their mothers preached to them as young children, such as: "If you can't say anything nice, don't say anything at all"; "Respect your elders"; and "Do unto others as you would have them do unto you." What this pair is striving for, however, is a bit deeper than what mom preached. "One act of kindness can result in millions of people being touched," according to former Abilene (Texas) *Reporter-News* newspaper editor and author Glenn Dromgoole. "I don't think it's so much random acts as it is intentional acts."

2   Dromgoole was inspired to contact Georgia author Alan Gibson after reading his book, *Priceless Gifts: Simple Ways to Make a Difference in the Lives of Others,* and finding they had common outlooks on life. As their friendship grew, they decided to co-found Americans for More Civility, which they

describe as a "nonpartisan, grass-roots movement advocating strength through reason, kindness, and generosity in public life and private actions." They started generating interest with a letter-writing campaign to newspapers across the nation, reminding people that the greatest gift humans can give one another is good behavior and politeness, in other words, civility.

3   Universities such as Harvard, Johns Hopkins, and the University of California agree the pair may be onto something. All three universities have commenced[1] programs and studies looking into civility and how it affects society. These schools are taking seriously Gibson's contention[2] that "Without civility this society does not work, no matter how splendid your constitutional guarantees are. With civility your society does work."

4   "Civility to me isn't about being gushy," Gibson says. "It's not about being nice, and it's not about smiling all the time. It's about a deeper kind of sustenance[3] that people can give to one another." Civility may be about inviting a co-worker who normally eats alone to lunch, keeping your word, introducing two people who would have never met or avoiding taking a cheap shot at a vulnerable[4] target. Gibson continues, "Look at some of the metaphors we have for dealing with one another: dog-eat-dog, swimming with sharks. I don't want to live that way. You win by giving as many gifts as you can, and you can do it in ways that don't involve a checkbook."

5   While Gibson and Dromgoole believe we are living in a world that often breeds incivility and almost promotes it as a way of life, journalist and Columbia University U.S. history graduate student Beverly Gage says there's no such crisis. "Civility is merely a topic that pops up in American history when the 'have-nots' are not acting the part the 'haves' want them to play."

6   "Essentially I think the movement toward civility on its face is not a bad thing," she contends. "My problem with a lot of what I have seen written about civility is it tends to overlook class. A lot of complaints about uncivil people are about working-class people." For example, Dromgoole says something must be "askew"[5] when a show such as *Jerry Springer* tops the TV ratings charts. Ms. Gage rebuts[6] that no one would expect to see a graduate of Harvard or Yale on "Jerry Springer," but it is often graduates from Ivy League colleges who point to people on such shows as "social misfits."

---

[1] **commenced**   began, started

[2] **contention**   assertion, belief, opinion

[3] **sustenance**   food, nourishment, support

[4] **vulnerable**   defenseless, weak, helpless

[5] **askew**   awry, off base, out of line

[6] **rebuts**   argues, refutes

7   In reviewing Harvard professor Stephen L. Carter's book, *Civility*, Ms. Gage writes, "In the bad attitudes of America's service employees, politicians, and urbanites, Carter has uncovered an 'incivility crisis' that threatens to rend our social fabric. While he's aware that his complaints sound suspiciously like those expressed by worried elites[7] throughout history, he maintains that 'this time we might be right.'"

8   President of the San Francisco Theological Seminary and author of *Say Please, Say Thank You: The Respect We Owe Our Mother*, Donald McCullough says getting back to the basics is essential to dealing with today's larger societal issues. "Our character is built one small brick at a time. Who we are is shaped in these little acts of courtesy or lack of courtesy that we extend to one another each day."

9   It's that courtesy that is lacking in many people's lives, according to Gibson and Dromgoole, who through their organization have found a real hunger among people for a kind word or deed. "When you emerge as the world's only superpower, there comes with it an obligation to be the world's most civilized people. It seems to me that America has done a lot of great things, and now that our era of winning world wars is hopefully over, we have the opportunity to civilize ourselves."

EXERCISE 2   Questions About the Reading

Select the letter that best completes each question or statement.

1.   The passage is about

   A.   listening to what mothers say about good manners.

   B.   starting an organization called Americans for More Civility.

   C.   being nice and smiling at people.

   D.   behaving in a way that shows concern for others.

2.   Choose the sentence that tells the main idea.

   A.   Gibson and Dromgoole decided to co-found Americans for More Civility, a grass roots movement advocating strength through reason, kindness, and generosity in public life and private actions.

   B.   The greatest gift humans can give one another is good behavior and politeness, in other words, civility.

---

[7] **elites**   advantaged people, leaders

C. Without civility this society does not work, no matter how splendid your constitutional guarantees are.

D. When you emerge as the world's only superpower, there comes with it an obligation to be the world's most civilized people.

3. Which of the following is *not* another definition for civility?

A. supporting one another

B. giving as many gifts as you can

C. providing little acts of courtesy

D. swimming with sharks

4. Which of the following is most likely true?

A. Most mothers are unconcerned with civility and public behavior.

B. A letter from Americans for More Civility appeared in a newspaper in your state.

C. Beverly Gage enjoys watching *The Jerry Springer Show* on television.

D. America's service employees, politicians, and urbanites generally promote civility.

5. The author mentions that Dromgoole was inspired to contact Georgia author Alan Gibson after reading his book, *Priceless Gifts: Simple Ways to Make a Difference in the Lives of Others,* to show that

A. Gibson and Dromgoole had similar interests.

B. Alan Gibson had used a catchy book title.

C. gifts do not have to be expensive or cost any money at all.

D. Dromgoole wanted Gibson to work for the *Reporter-News* in Abilene, Texas.

6. As used in the sentence, "Our *character* is built one small brick at a time. Who we are is shaped in these little acts of courtesy or lack of courtesy that we extend to one another each day," the word *character* does *not* mean

A. physique.

B. spirit.

C. moral fiber.

D. nature.

EXERCISE 3   Sentence Explication

1. Either use the sentence that follows, or select and copy a different sentence from the reading selection.

   You win by giving as many gifts as you can, and you can do it in ways that don't involve a checkbook.   paragraph #4

   Or the sentence you choose:

   _____

   _____

                                                          paragraph # ___

2. Paraphrase the sentence by rewriting it in your own words.

   _____

   _____

   _____

   _____

3. React to the sentence. What comments and questions do you have about it?

   _____

   _____

   _____

   _____

4. Relate to the sentence. What personal experiences does it bring to mind?

   _____

   _____

   _____

   _____

EXERCISE 4   Questions for Writing and Discussion

1. What did the founders of the letter-writing campaign say was "the greatest gift humans can give one another"? Why do the writers believe as they do?

2. Donald McCullough said, "Who we are is shaped in these little acts of courtesy or lack of courtesy that we extend to one another each day." What is the meaning of McCullough's statement?

3. Is civility an issue related to gender, age, or social/economic class? Explain.

Working from Sentences to Paragraph

Rearrange Sentences with New Beginnings

Peace can not be kept by force.
It can only be won, through understanding.

— Albert Einstein (1879–1955)

EXERCISE 5   Promoting Civility at School

Part A

Use the provided new sentence beginnings to change the emphasis of the following sentences describing projects that promote safe schools. As you rearrange the words, be sure to keep the meaning of the original sentence.

1. Interpersonal violence among youth is a major problem across the United States.

    A major problem _____

    _____

    _____

2. Violence has become a more prevalent concern for society, and safety at school is an issue.

Because _____

_____

_____

3. Projects have been developed in schools across the United States to reduce interpersonal violence among youth.

Schools across the United States _____

_____

_____

4. Conflict resolution and peer mediation (CR/PM) training are implemented to help improve behavioral and social skills.

The implementation _____

_____

_____

5. An entire class or school is taught conflict resolution by skilled personnel.

Skilled personnel _____

_____

_____

6. A few selected students are provided peer mediation training so that they can help resolve disagreements.

Peer mediation training _____

_____

_____

7. Conflict resolution projects teach students to manage anger, control aggressive responses, and avoid potentially violent confrontations.

   Students learn _____

   _____

   _____

8. Conflict resolution and peer mediation allow students to settle disagreements peacefully among themselves.

   Using conflict resolution _____

   _____

   _____

Part B

After checking your rearranged sentences with your instructor, copy them to create a paragraph.

If you become self-centered, you will build a wall around yourself and lose your freedom. If you can humble yourself in preparation for an event, you will surely be better able to judge and understand it.

— Kyuzo Mifune

Combine Sentences with New Beginnings

EXERCISE 6   The Discipline of the Dojo

Part A

Read the following draft of an informative paragraph explaining the required behavior in studying the martial arts.

The students enter the dojo or training room. The students stop chewing gum and listening to the radio. The students stop any other distracting behaviors. The students change into training uniforms. This change helps them forget outside concerns. This change helps them focus on their task. The students walk to the practice mat. They bow. This action expresses intent to concentrate on the training. This behavior reminds students to be grateful for the chance to train. Some students arrive late. They must stand quietly just outside the mat. The instructor invites the students to join in. These students kneel at the back of the class. These students meditate to calm their minds. These students join the warm-up. The instructor speaks to the class. The students kneel politely. Students bow to their partners when practice begins. Students bow to their partners when practice ends. To talk on the mat during class is impolite. To talk interferes with the concentration of other students. The class ends. The students quickly line up. They kneel in front of the instructor. The students stand only when the instructor has left the room. They find their partners. They bow to each of them. They thank them for being partners in the training.

Part B

Combine the ideas from the sentences in each group to write one new sentence. Begin the new sentence using the indicated words. As you write the sentence, think about the emphasis and relationships you want to achieve.

1.

The students enter the dojo or training room.

The students stop chewing gum and listening to the radio.

The students stop any other distracting behaviors.

When students _____

_____

_____

2.

The students change into training uniforms.

This change helps them forget outside concerns.

This change helps them focus on their task.

Changing into _____

_____

_____

_____

3.

The students walk to the practice mat.

They bow.

This action reminds students to be grateful for the chance to train.

After walking _____

_____

_____

_____

4.

Some students arrive late.

They must stand quietly just outside the mat.

The instructor invites the students to join in.

Students who _____

_____

_____

_____

5.

These students kneel at the back of the class.

These students meditate to calm their minds.

These students join the warm-up.

Before _____

_____

_____

6.

The instructor speaks to the class.

The students kneel politely.

The students kneel _____

_____

_____

7.

Students bow to their partners when practice begins.

Students bow to their partners when practice ends.

When practice _____

_____

_____

8.

To talk on the mat during class is impolite.

To talk interferes with the concentration of other students.

Talking _____

_____

_____

9.

The class ends.

The students quickly line up.

They kneel in front of the instructor.

Students _____

_____

_____

Part C

After checking your combined sentences with your instructor, copy them to create a paragraph. Note the differences between the original and the rewritten paragraphs.

Combine Sentences on Your Own

Nothing more rapidly inclines a person to go into a monastery than reading a book on etiquette. There are so many trivial ways in which it is possible to commit some social sin.

— Quentin Crisp (b. 1908)

EXERCISE 7   Rules for Dating

Part A

Read the following draft of an informative paragraph about the rigid requirements of dating during the 1800s.

During the nineteenth century a young lady was prepared for marriage. She was trained in the arts. She learned the rules of socializing with young men. She was instructed to look for a man. This man was to be unselfish. This man was to be hardworking. This man was to be five years older than she was. There were good places to meet potential husbands. One place was a church supper. Another place was a holiday ball. Sometimes a man wanted to meet a lady. He found a mutual friend. This friend could arrange introductions. Many women wrote letters to their suitors. They sent lockets, coins, portraits, poems, and locks of hair. A Victorian[1] gentleman proposed to a woman. Then she accepted. This was the time for the man to ask her parents' approval.

Part B

Revise the paragraph by combining the ideas from the sentences in each group to write one new sentence. As you write each sentence, think about the emphasis and relationships you want to achieve, adding transitions as needed.

1.

During the nineteenth century a young lady was prepared for marriage.

~~She was~~ trained in the arts.

She learned the rules of socializing with young men.

_____

_____

_____

2.

She was instructed to look for a man.

This man was to be unselfish.

This man was to be hardworking.

This man was to be five years older than she was.

_____

_____

_____

[1] **Victorian**   belonging to the age of Queen Victoria of Great Britain in the nineteenth century

3.

There were good places to meet potential husbands.

One place was a church supper.

Another place was a holiday ball.

_____

_____

_____

4.

Sometimes a man wanted to meet a lady.

He had to find a mutual friend.

This friend could arrange introductions.

_____

_____

_____

5.

Many women wrote letters to their suitors.

They sent lockets, coins, portraits, poems, and locks of hair.

_____

_____

_____

6.

A Victorian gentleman proposed to a woman.

Then she accepted.

This was the time for the man to ask her parents' approval.

_____

_____

_____

Part C

After you have checked your sentences with your instructor, copy them to create a paragraph. Note the differences between the original and the rewritten paragraphs.

Identify Sentences in Context

Sports do not build character. They reveal it.
— Heywood Hale Broun (1888–1939)

EXERCISE 8   Good Sports for Life

The following paragraph about sportsmanship is missing periods. Add a period to mark the end of a sentence and capitalize the beginning word of the next sentence. Copy on the adjacent numbered line each word you have capitalized.

When superstar athletes misbehave, their antics make headlines and TV news not surprisingly, bad sportsmanship increases at other levels of play athletes may hear that winning isn't everything, but their behavior often is based on a win-at-all-costs attitude athletes who are good sports play by the rules, respect opponents and officials, and value hard work over outcome when opponents get injured during a game, good sports show respect by clapping for them as they get up to leave the game good sports cheer for an opposing team that makes a skillful play they don't blame losses on the officials, the weather, faulty

1. _____
2. _____
3. _____
4. _____
5. _____
6. _____
7. _____
8. _____
9. _____
10. _____
11. _____
12. _____

equipment, or some other factor after the game, they
congratulate both teams and coaches for their efforts
success means trying hard, not necessarily winning
since most people, like most athletes, are not always
winners, learning about good sportsmanship is one of
life's most important lessons.

13. _____
14. _____
15. _____
16. _____
17. _____
18. _____

Rearrange and Combine Sentences Using Transitions

Manners are a sensitive awareness of the feelings of others. If you have that awareness, you have good manners, no matter what fork you use.

— Emily Post (1872–1960)

EXERCISE 9   What to Do at Meals

Part A

Read a draft of an informative paragraph about table manners. In Parts B and C, you will work on combining, rearranging, and adding transitions to make the paragraph coherent.

Using appropriate manners during a formal meal can be important. A formal meal may be part of an interview, a business conference, or a wedding reception. Napkins are unfolded. Napkins are placed on the lap. Proper posture at the table is desirable. A diner should not lean back against the chair. A diner should not lean forward with elbows on the table. Unpleasant discussions are inappropriate at mealtime. Arguments are inappropriate at mealtime. People at the table should wait to begin eating. They should wait until all are served. Talking and chewing at the same time is inconsiderate of others at the table. Using a straw to slurp a beverage is also inconsiderate. "Please pass the salt" has a meaning. It means to move both the salt and the pepper shakers. A person can learn more about table manners.

Books tell about table manners. Courses teach about table manners. Sites on the Internet explain table manners.

Part B

Revise the paragraph by using rearrangement, combining, and transitions *wherever appropriate* to create new sentences. Not every sentence needs to be rewritten.

1. Using appropriate manners during a formal meal can be important.

2. A formal meal may be part of an interview, a business conference, or a wedding reception.

3. Napkins are to be unfolded.

4. Napkins are placed on the lap.

5. Proper posture at the table is desirable.

6. A diner should not lean back against the chair.

7. A diner should not lean forward with elbows on the table.

8. Unpleasant discussions are inappropriate at mealtime.

9. Arguments are inappropriate at mealtime.

10. People at the table should wait to begin eating.

11. They should wait until all are served.

12. Talking and chewing at the same time is inconsiderate.

13. Using a straw to slurp a beverage is also inconsiderate.

14. "Please pass the salt" has a meaning.

15. It means to move both the salt and the pepper shakers.

16. A person can learn more about table manners.

17. Books tell about table manners.

18. Courses teach about table manners.

19. Sites on the Internet explain table manners.

Part C

After you have checked your sentences with your instructor, copy them to create a paragraph. Note the differences between the original and the rewritten paragraphs.

Writing from Experience

EXERCISE 10 Write a Paragraph

Write a paragraph of 8–12 sentences on one of the following topics.

1. In a community there are accepted rules for many kinds of behavior. Choose an aspect of your life and explain the rules for doing the activity appropriately. You may want to give rules for dating, for a classroom, for an employee at your place of work, for home.

   Questions to Consider

   What is the situation for which you are giving rules?

   What is your involvement in the situation?

   What are the rules?

   What are the reasons for the rules?

   Are the rules helpful in the situation?

2. Have you been involved in or witnessed a potentially hostile or a destructive situation based on a disagreement between people? If so, write about the situation.

   Questions to Consider

   What was the disagreement?

   Where and when did it occur?

Who was involved? In what way were you involved?

How was the dispute resolved?

What did you learn from the experience?

3. Explain what good manners you practice and how you learned them. Or, explain what manners are important for children and how they should be taught these manners.

Questions to Consider

What manners are involved?

How does the person demonstrate the manners?

Why are the manners important?

How did the person learn or teach them?

4. Peacemakers have important roles in human interactions. Tell about a time that you were a peacemaker.

Questions to Consider

What was the situation?

Who was involved?

What happened to cause a problem?

What did you do to bring peace to the situation?

How did the others in the group react to what you did?

For question 5, you are on your own to write your own questions for development.

5. Participation in or watching a sport can be a time to observe behavior. Tell about a time you either played in a game or watched a game during which a person or a group of people demonstrated civility or good sportsmanship.

Questions for Development

_____

_____

_____

_____

For question 6, you are on your own to create a focus as well as write your own questions for development.

6.   Write on a topic related to civility.

Focus

_____

Questions for Development

_____

_____

_____

_____

EXERCISE 11   Revise Your Paragraph

Part A
Reread the paragraph you wrote for Exercise 10.

1.   Choose one sentence to rearrange.

Original Sentence _____

_____

Rearranged Sentence _____

_____

2.   Choose two or more sentences that could be effectively combined.

Original Sentences

_____

_____

_____

_____

Combined Sentence

_____

_____

_____

You may want to use these revised sentences in the final draft of your paragraph.

Part B
Check your paragraph before submitting your final draft.

A CLEAR TOPIC SENTENCE
❐   Does the topic sentence state the topic?

❐   Does the topic sentence state what you will tell about the topic?

CONVINCING SUPPORT
❐   Do your sentences say what you want them to mean?

❐   Have you included enough details to make your ideas clear?

EFFECTIVE ORGANIZATION
❐   Does the paragraph have a beginning, a middle, and an end?

❐   Does your concluding sentence provide a summary of your main idea?

❐   Do you use transitions to link your ideas?

SUCCESSFUL SENTENCES
❐   Is each sentence complete?

❐   Have you eliminated run-ons, fused sentences, and fragments?

❐   Have you written each word you need?

❐   Have you used a spell checker, speller, or dictionary to be sure words are spelled correctly?

❐   Have you used the correct form of homonyms?

EFFECTIVE TITLE
❐   Does your title suggest what the paragraph is about? Does the title make someone want to read your paragraph?

Writing from Resources

EXERCISE 12   Share Information

To answer these questions, visit the library or use a search engine on the Internet, such as Lycos, Yahoo, or AltaVista. As you write your answers, use sentence rearrangement and combining techniques.

Your instructor will explain how to complete this section regarding the number of questions to answer and whether to work independently, with a partner, or in a group.

Promoting Civility at School

1. What is peer mediation in education? What training is provided for the peer mentors?

2. What is divorce mediation?

3. What kinds of disagreements are handled by small-claims court?

4. What is the Golden Rule or the Role of Reciprocity? How is it stated in three of the world's major religions?

5. What suggestions do pediatricians and counselors have for teaching children how to deal with anger?

6. What suggestions do professional counselors offer adults who want to learn to deal with anger?

The Discipline of the Dojo

7. What are the martial arts? Where did they originate? What philosophy of life do they support?

8. What is involved in one of the following martial arts: judo, jujitsu, karate, kick boxing, kung fu, tae kwon do, tai chi?

9.   What is a dojo? How is it set up? What equipment is provided?

10.   What is a black belt? What does a student of the martial arts do to earn one?

11.   What is sumo wrestling?

Rules for Dating

12.   What are the qualities of a diamond? What distinguishes the finest diamonds?

13.   Explain the customs of an American wedding or a wedding in another culture.

14.   What is the significance of each of the following: chaperone, dowry, shower, fiancé/fiancée, best man, bridesmaid, matron of honor, throwing rice, throwing the bridal bouquet?

Good Sports for Life

15.   How have women's sports evolved since the 1970s? What is the Federal Educational Amendment Title 9?

16.   How can a person become a sports official?

17.   What are the guidelines for participants and spectators in interscholastic leagues at your school or another college in the United States?

What to Do at Meals

18.   How does a person with good manners eat an artichoke, a lobster, a bowl of soup, a plate of spaghetti, and a piece of watermelon?

19.   What is the origin of eating utensils? What are the differences between the American and the European or continental style of using utensils?

20.   What are considered good manners for using a napkin, fork, spoon, and knife?

21.   What are considered good table manners in another country?

22.   What is the origin of the Japanese tea ceremony? What is involved?

More About Civility

23. Read George Washington's *Rules for Civility.* Tell when and why Washington wrote these rules. Copy three of the rules and explain why they are no longer relevant. Copy three of the rules and explain why they are helpful today.

24. What is appropriate etiquette in communicating with someone who is in a wheelchair, is blind, or has difficulty hearing or speaking?

25. What are good manners in using e-mail and other features of cyberspace?

EXERCISE 13 Understand Idioms

What is the meaning of each of the following idioms related to civility? To find the meaning, check a dictionary or a specialized idiom dictionary, or ask someone who understands the idiom to explain it to you.

man of his word

as good as his word

actions speak louder than words

saving grace

make a virtue out of necessity

swallow one's pride

kill with kindness

two wrongs don't make a right

rob Peter to pay Paul

mind your p's and q's

talk with a forked tongue

CHAPTER 6

Attire

Costly thy habit as thy purse can buy,
But not expressed in fancy; rich not gaudy;
For the apparel oft proclaims the man.

— William Shakespeare (1564–1616)

To study clothing is to learn about history, science, and culture. The reading in this chapter is about the special attire worn by astronauts.

Connecting Reading with Writing

EXERCISE 1 Reflections on Attire

1. What are some of the problems that have to be overcome in order to travel in space?

   _____

   _____

2. What are some of the benefits that can be derived from space travel and exploration?

   _____

   _____

   _____

   _____

Wardrobe for Space

from National Aeronautics and Space Administration *FACTS*

1   To be able to explore and work in space, humans have to take their environment with them because there is no atmosphere to supply the pressure and oxygen necessary to support life. Inside the spacecraft, the atmosphere can be controlled so that special clothing isn't needed, but when outside, humans need the protection of a spacesuit.

2   Earth's atmosphere is 20 percent oxygen and 80 percent nitrogen from sea level to about 75 miles up, where space begins. At 18,000 feet, the atmosphere is half as dense as it is on the ground, and at altitudes above 40,000 feet, air is so thin and the amount of oxygen so small that pressure oxygen masks no longer do the job. Above the 63,000-foot threshold,

humans must wear spacesuits that supply oxygen for breathing and that maintain a pressure around the body to keep body fluids in the liquid state. At this altitude the total air pressure is no longer sufficient to keep body fluids from boiling.

3   The air we breathe normally has about 20 percent oxygen and exerts a pressure of 15 pounds per square inch (psi) on our bodies. Spacesuits for the space shuttle era are pressurized at only 4.3 pounds per square inch (psi), but because the gas in the suit is 100 percent oxygen instead of 20 percent, the person in a spacesuit actually has more oxygen to breathe than is available at sea level without the spacesuit. Before leaving the space shuttle to perform tasks in space, an astronaut has to spend several hours breathing pure oxygen and then proceed into space. This procedure is necessary to remove nitrogen dissolved in body fluids and thereby to prevent its release as gas bubbles into the bloodstream when pressure is reduced, a condition commonly called "the bends."

4   The spacesuit also shields the astronaut from deadly hazards. Besides providing protection from bombardment by micrometeoroids, the spacesuit insulates the wearer from the temperature extremes of space. Without the Earth's atmosphere to filter the sunlight, the side of the suit facing the Sun can be heated to a temperature as high as 250 degrees Fahrenheit, while the other side, exposed to darkness of deep space, can get as cold as –250 degrees Fahrenheit.

5   Astronauts of the space shuttle era have more than one wardrobe for space flight, and what they wear depends on the job they are doing. During the launch and re-entry, the astronauts wear a partially pressurized suit and a parachute pack. The suit has a helmet, gloves, and boots which all serve as protection for the astronaut. Within the suit are bladders that automatically fill with air at reduced cabin pressures. At low atmospheric pressures, the blood will pool in the lower body, causing the astronaut to black out. The air bladders in the suit maintain the pressure on the lower body to prevent this from happening.

6   During orbit, astronauts work inside the space shuttle in shirt-sleeve comfort. Prior to a mission, crew members are outfitted from a selection of clothing including flight suits, trousers, lined zipper jackets, knit shirts, sleep shorts, soft slippers, and underwear. The materials of every component of the clothing are flame retardant. Covering the exterior of the garments are closable pockets for storing such items as pens, pencils, data books, sunglasses, a multipurpose Swiss army pocketknife, and scissors.

7   While working outside of the shuttle during a mission, astronauts wear an extravehicular mobility unit (EMU). This suit has interchangeable parts so it

can be assembled to fit different astronauts. This makes the suit more cost effective since it can be reused. The EMU has a liquid cooling garment, which is a one-piece suit made of spandex, and keeps the astronaut cool while in the suit. The unit also contains headphones and microphones, a drink bag that carries water, a life support system containing oxygen, and a urine collection device. Gloves are included with the unit along with a helmet and a visor. All of this is necessary to protect the astronaut from micrometeoroids, solar radiation, infrared radiation, temperature changes, pressure changes, and oxygen deprivation.

8   To help the astronaut get around freely while performing a space walk, a manned maneuvering unit (MMU) can be attached to the EMU. The MMU is a nitrogen-propelled backpack that allows the astronaut to fly with precision. The MMU has a 35mm camera attached to it so that the astronaut can take pictures while in flight.

9   Sophisticated technologies and enormous amounts of resources are employed to develop highly functional space suits. In the future, space suits are expected to become less costly and even more functional than those currently being used. Space suits will ultimately be able to provide astronauts with a more comfortable working environment and an ease of movement similar to that experienced on Earth.

EXERCISE 2   Questions About the Reading

Select the letter that best completes each question or statement.

1.   This passage is mostly about outer space and

   A.   technology.

   B.   astronauts.

   C.   space wardrobe.

   D.   body fluids.

2.   Choose the sentence that tells the main idea.

   A.   What astronauts wear on a mission is determined by the job they are doing.

   B.   When outside in space, astronauts need the protection of a spacesuit.

   C.   Astronauts work inside the space shuttle in shirt-sleeve comfort.

   D.   Future space suits will provide astronauts with an environment similar to Earth's.

3. The bladders of a partial pressure suit automatically fill with air at reduced cabin pressures

   A. to make it easier for the astronauts to breathe.

   B. to provide a space for urination.

   C. to prevent the astronaut from blacking out.

   D. to increase the astronaut's oxygen supply.

4. Based on the article, which of the following is likely to be true?

   A. Because the Earth's atmosphere directs the sunlight, there are no extreme temperatures on Earth.

   B. Before the invention of the MMU, astronauts were not able to move about in space.

   C. By the end of the twenty-first century, astronauts will not need to wear space suits.

   D. Space garments need closable pockets since small objects might otherwise float away in the microgravity environment.

5. The author mentions protecting the astronaut from micrometeoroids, solar radiation, infrared radiation, temperature changes, pressure changes, and oxygen deprivation to explain

   A. the differences between Earth and outer space.

   B. why space suits have interchangeable parts.

   C. why the MMU has a 35mm camera attached to it.

   D. the dangers in the environment of outer space.

6. As used in the sentence, "Sophisticated technologies and enormous amounts of resources are *employed* to develop highly functional space suits," the word *employed* means

   A. spent.

   B. labored.

   C. utilized.

   D. worked.

EXERCISE 3   Sentence Explication

1. Either use the sentence that follows, or select and copy a different sentence from the reading selection.

    Astronauts of the space shuttle have more than one wardrobe for space flight, and what they wear depends on the job they are doing.

    paragraph #5

    Or the sentence you choose:

    _____

    _____

    paragraph #____

2. Paraphrase the sentence by rewriting it in your own words.

    _____

    _____

    _____

    _____

3. React to the sentence. What comments and questions do you have about it?

    _____

    _____

    _____

    _____

4. Relate to the sentence. What personal experiences does it bring to mind?

    _____

    _____

_____

_____

_____

EXERCISE 4   Questions for Writing and Discussion

1. What protection does a space suit provide an astronaut?

2. For astronauts, what problems are caused by a decrease in oxygen and air pressure outside Earth's atmosphere?

3. In addition to a space suit, what other outfits does an astronaut need? For what purpose is each outfit used?

Working from Sentences to Paragraph

Rearrange Sentences with New Beginnings

EXERCISE 5   The Cowboy's Uniform

Part A

Use the provided new sentence beginnings to change the emphasis of the following sentences about Americans' early television hero, the cowboy. As you rearrange the words, be sure to keep the meaning of the original sentence.

1. The American cowboy was an imposing[1] figure riding the cattle trails across the Great Plains.

   _As_ _____

   _____

   _____

[1] **imposing**   impressive, as by virtue of size, bearing, or power

2. Covering him from head to foot, the cowboy's outfit served as a protective uniform.

   The cowboy's outfit covered him _____

   _____

   _____

3. A colorful bandana was tied around his neck.

   Tied around his neck _____

   _____

   _____

4. He pulled the bandana over his face to keep off trail dust or stuffed it into his hat to insulate the top of his head.

   To keep off trail dust _____

   _____

   _____

5. His shirt was collarless and made of cotton or flannel.

   He wore _____

   _____

   _____

6. Buckskin sewn over the seat and inner thighs prevented his pants from fraying against the saddle.

   Sewn _____

   _____

   _____

7. The cowboy liked to wear his pants tight around the waist to make sure they stayed up.

   Because _____

   _____

   _____

8. They soaked their blue jeans in a horse watering trough and then laid them out in the sun to shrink dry.

   After soaking _____

   _____

   _____

9. One possession every cowboy prized was a broad-brimmed hat.

   A broad-brimmed hat _____

   _____

   _____

10. The cowboy's hat was used to fan a fire or to carry water.

    The cowboy _____

    _____

    _____

11. A cowboy hated to take off his hat, so he ignored etiquette by wearing it indoors.

    Hating _____

    _____

    _____

Part B

After checking your rearranged sentences with your instructor, copy them to create a paragraph.

Combine Sentences with New Beginnings

Necessity is the mother of invention.

— Anonymous

EXERCISE 6   Blue Jeans—An American Classic

Part A

Read the following draft of a paragraph about the origins of an American garment that captured the world market. In Parts B and C, you will work on combining sentences and adding transitions to make the paragraph coherent.

Americans have a number one clothing favorite. Their favorite is denim blue jeans. These rugged pants were first made by Levi Strauss. Levi Strauss was an immigrant to the United States from Bavaria[1] in 1847. Levi moved to San Francisco. Levi started a dry goods business in San Francisco. This was during the Gold Rush in the 1850s. Miners were digging for gold. Miners needed rugged clothing. Levi went into business with Jacob Davis. This happened in 1872. Jacob Davis was a tailor from Nevada. Jacob Davis was talented. Davis made denim pants more durable. Davis inserted metal rivets[2] at points of strain. Metal rivets were placed at the pocket corners. Metal rivets prevented the weight of tools splitting open the pockets. Another metal rivet was placed at the bottom of the fly. This stopped the crotch seam from splitting open. This could happen when a miner squatted to pan for gold. Miners in the West wanted denim pants. Ranchers in the West wanted denim pants. Levi opened two factories. Levi's jeans became a multimillion-dollar industry. Jeans became the symbol of the American garment.

---

[1] **Bavaria**   a region in southern Germany

[2] **rivets**   metal pins inserted through holes in the pieces to be joined

Part B

Combine the ideas from the sentences in each group to write one new sentence. Begin the new sentence using the indicated words. As you write the sentence, think about the emphasis and relationships you want to achieve.

1.

Americans have a number one clothing favorite.

Their favorite is denim blue jeans.

The number one _____

_____

_____

_____

2.

These rugged pants were first made by Levi Strauss.

Levi Strauss was an immigrant to the United States from Bavaria in 1847.

Levi Strauss _____

_____

_____

_____

3.

Levi moved to San Francisco.

Levi started a dry goods business in San Francisco.

This was during the Gold Rush in the 1850s.

During the Gold Rush _____

_____

_____

_____

4.

Miners were digging for gold.

Miners needed rugged clothing.

Miners _____

_____

_____

_____

5.

Levi went into business with Jacob Davis.

This happened in 1872.

Jacob Davis was a tailor from Nevada.

Jacob Davis was talented.

In 1872 _____

_____

_____

_____

6.

Davis made denim pants more durable.

Davis inserted metal rivets at points of strain.

By inserting metal rivets _____

_____

_____

_____

7.

Metal rivets were placed at the pocket corners.

Metal rivets prevented the weight of tools splitting open the pockets.

Metal rivets _____

_____

_____

_____

8.

Another metal rivet was placed at the bottom of the fly.

This stopped the crotch seam from splitting open.

This could happen when a miner squatted to pan for gold.

Placed at the bottom of the fly _____

_____

_____

_____

9.

Miners in the West wanted denim pants.

Ranchers in the West wanted denim pants.

Levi opened two factories.

Miners _____

_____

_____

_____

10.

Levi's jeans became a multimillion-dollar industry.

Jeans became the symbol of the American garment.

In time _____

_____

_____

_____

Part C

After checking your combined sentences with your instructor, copy them to create a paragraph. Add transitions to make the paragraph coherent. Note the differences between the original and the rewritten paragraphs.

Combine Sentences on Your Own

A stitch in time saves nine.

— proverb

EXERCISE 7   Thimble and Thread

Part A

Read the following draft of a descriptive paragraph about a time when clothes were made and remade at home. In Parts B and C, you will work on combining sentences and adding transitions to make the paragraph coherent.

Years ago training in needlework began early in a woman's life. Training in clothes construction began early in a woman's life. Young girls took care of much of the household sewing. Young girls took care of much of the household mending. They learned how to sew shirts and shifts.[1] They learned how to knit sweaters. They learned how to darn[2] "new footed" stockings. During the first half of the twentieth century, most homes had a sewing basket. The sewing basket was usually found next to the mother's chair. It contained spools of colored thread. It had several thimbles.[3] It had needles. It had scraps of fabric. Mending was a chore. The chore was ordinary. The chore was daily. The mother mended torn school clothes. She darned socks. She let down or took up dress hems. Boy's corduroy school pants were patched at the knees. Scraps of cloth were used. Frayed collars and cuffs on men's shirts were carefully detached. Frayed collars and cuffs were sewn back on with the worn part turned around. Today, old clothes are discarded. Socks with holes are discarded. Shirts with frayed[4] collars are discarded. In fact, many people are unfamiliar with using needle and thread. Many people need a tailor to sew on buttons.

Part B

Revise the paragraph by combining the ideas from the sentences in each group to write one new sentence. As you write each sentence, think about the emphasis and relationships you want to achieve, adding transitions as needed.

1.

Years ago, training in needlework began early in a woman's life.

Training in clothes construction began early in a woman's life.

_____

_____

_____

_____

[1] **shift**   a loose-fitting woman's dress

[2] **to darn**   to mend a garment by weaving thread or yarn across a gap or hole

[3] **thimble**   a small cup made of metal, ceramic, plastic, leather, or other hard material, worn for protection on the finger that pushes the needle in sewing

[4] **frayed**   well-worn, in holes

2.

Young girls took care of much of the household sewing.

Young girls care of much of the household mending.

_____

_____

_____

_____

3.

They learned how to sew shirts and shifts.

They learned how to knit sweaters.

They learned how to darn "new footed" stockings.

_____

_____

_____

_____

4.

During the first half of the twentieth century, most homes had a sewing basket.

The sewing basket was usually found next to the mother's chair.

_____

_____

_____

_____

5.

The sewing basket contained spools of colored thread.

The sewing basket had several thimbles.

The sewing basket had needles.

The sewing basket had scraps of fabric.

_____

_____

_____

_____

6.

Mending was a chore.

The chore was ordinary.

The chore was daily.

_____

_____

_____

_____

7.

The mother mended torn school clothes.

She darned socks.

She let down or took up dress hems.

_____

_____

_____

_____

8.

Boy's corduroy school pants were patched at the knees.

Scraps of cloth were used.

_____

_____

_____

_____

9.

Frayed collars and cuffs on men's shirts were carefully detached.

Frayed collars and cuffs were sewn back on with the worn part turned around.

_____

_____

_____

_____

10.

Today, old clothes are discarded.

Socks with holes are discarded.

Shirts with frayed collars are discarded.

_____

_____

_____

_____

11.

In fact, many people are unfamiliar with using needle and thread.

Many people need a tailor to sew on buttons.

_____

_____

_____

_____

Part C

After you have checked your sentences with your instructor, copy them to create a coherent paragraph. Note the differences between the original and the rewritten paragraphs.

Identify Sentences in Context

> *. . . they sewed fig leaves together and made themselves aprons.*
>
> — Genesis 3:7

EXERCISE 8 Aprons—A Style for Every Need

The following paragraph about protective clothing used by many workers is missing periods. Add a period to mark the end of a sentence and capitalize the beginning word of the next sentence. Copy on the adjacent numbered line each word you have capitalized.

An apron is a garment usually fastened in the back
and worn over the front of the body to safeguard
clothing many women wear this piece of clothing
with pride as a symbol of nurturing, homemaking,

1. _____

2. _____

3. _____

4. _____

and motherhood some women, however, consider the	5. _____
apron to represent restriction and repression men,	6. _____
too, in their work as blacksmiths, ticket sellers, and	7. _____
other occupations have worn aprons today, both men	8. _____
and women use aprons as waiters, carpenters, bakers,	9. _____
clowns, magicians, merchants, and butchers patients	10. _____
having x-rays wear lead aprons apron makers sell	11. _____
their products in a variety of fabrics, styles, colors,	12. _____
and with many pockets as a tribute to aprons, a group	13. _____
of fiber-and-needle artists from all walks of life have	14. _____
created their own versions of the apron to showcase	15. _____
the universal cover-up.	16. _____

Rearrange and Combine Sentences Using Transitions

Every fashion goes out of style.

— Japanese proverb

EXERCISE 9   The Necktie—A Link to the Past

Part A

Read a draft of an informative paragraph about the origin of men's neckties. In Parts B and C, you will work on combining, rearranging, and adding transitions to make the paragraph coherent.

Men's neckties became fashionable in the seventeenth century. Soldiers from Croatia were visiting Paris. The soldiers wore scarves around their necks. The scarves were made of brightly colored silk. King Louis XIV of France liked the look of the scarves. The king created a royal troop. The king required the royal troop to wear cravats. The king named the troop Royal Cravattes. *Cravattes* is derived from the word "Croatia." In time, the cravat or necktie became an important part of a man's wardrobe. There were many necktie styles. There were tasseled strings, plaid scarves, lace, and embroidered linen. Ties were knotted in one hundred different ways. By the end of the twentieth century, fashions changed. Fewer men were wearing neckties.

Part B

Revise the paragraph by using rearrangement, combining, and transitions *wherever appropriate* to create new sentences. Not every sentence needs to be rewritten.

1. Men's neckties became fashionable in the seventeenth century.

2. Soldiers from Croatia were visiting Paris.

3. The soldiers wore scarves around their necks.

4. The scarves were made of brightly colored silk.

5. King Louis XIV of France liked the look of the scarves.

6. The king created a royal troop.

7. The king required the royal troop to wear cravats.

8. The king named the troop Royal Cravattes.

9. Cravattes is derived from the word "Croatia."

10. In time, the cravat or necktie became an important part of a man's wardrobe.

11. There were many necktie styles.

12. There were tasseled strings, plaid scarves, lace, and embroidered linen.

13. Ties were knotted in one hundred different ways.

14. By the end of the twentieth century, fashions changed.

15. Fewer men were wearing neckties.

Part C

After you have checked your sentences with your instructor, copy them to create a paragraph. Note the differences between the original and the rewritten paragraphs.

Writing from Experience

EXERCISE 10   Write a Paragraph

Write a paragraph of 8–12 sentences on one of the following topics.

1. Fashion changes from year to year. Some outfits, however, are especially memorable. Describe an outfit that left a lasting impression on you.

   Questions to Consider

   Who was wearing the outfit?

   When did you see or wear the outfit?

   What did the outfit look like?

   What kind of impression did it leave?

2. Today cloth and clothes are generally produced in a factory rather than made by hand. Many products, however, are still made by hand. Consider something that you, a family member, or a friend does by hand, such as making ice cream, cookies, or other foods; sewing or knitting clothes; building models; doing other projects or crafts.

   Questions to Consider

   What is the hand-made or handcrafted item?

   Who makes it?

   How did the person learn the craft?

   How does the item compare with a manufactured version?

3. Just as cowboys have special clothing and equipment to do their jobs, other workers today may have a job requiring special uniforms and/or tools. Write about a special uniform and/or tool.

Questions to Consider

What is the particular outfit or apparatus?

Who wears it or uses it?

What does it look like?

How well does the outfit or apparatus function?

Would you make any changes?

4. For holidays, religious and national observances, as well as other events, clothing or costumes often have special significance. Halloween parties, weddings, parades, and proms are a few of the occasions for which attire can be important. Describe an outfit that you wore for a festive occasion.

Questions to Consider

What was the celebration?

Where and when was the celebration?

What did you wear? (Describe your outfit.)

Where is the outfit now?

For question 5, you are on your own to create questions for development.

5. What does your wardrobe tell about you?

Questions for Development

_____

_____

_____

_____

_____

For question 6, you are on your own to decide a focus and to create questions for development.

6. Write on a topic of your choice about clothing.

    Focus

    _____

    Questions for Development

    _____

    _____

    _____

    _____

    _____

EXERCISE 11   Revise Your Paragraph

Part A

Reread the paragraph you wrote for Exercise 10.

1. Choose one sentence to rearrange.

    Original Sentence _____

    _____

    Rearranged Sentence _____

    _____

2. Choose two or more sentences that could be effectively combined.

    Original Sentences

    _____

    _____

_____

_____

Combined Sentence

_____

_____

_____

You may want to use these revised sentences in the final draft of your paragraph.

Part B

Check your paragraph for accurate punctuation and spelling. Be certain you have included transitions.

A CLEAR TOPIC SENTENCE

❒ Does the topic sentence state the topic?

❒ Does the topic sentence state what you will tell about the topic?

CONVINCING SUPPORT

❒ Do your sentences say what you want them to mean?

❒ Have you included enough details to make your ideas clear?

EFFECTIVE ORGANIZATION

❒ Does the paragraph have a beginning, a middle, and an end?

❒ Does your concluding sentence provide a summary of your main idea?

❒ Do you use transitions to link your ideas?

SUCCESSFUL SENTENCES

❒ Is each sentence complete?

❒ Have you eliminated run-ons and fragments?

❒ Have you written each word you need?

❒ Have you used a spell checker, speller, or dictionary to be sure words are spelled correctly?

❒ Have you used the correct form of homonyms?

EFFECTIVE TITLE

❐ Does your title suggest what the paragraph is about and make someone interested in reading it?

Writing from Resources

EXERCISE 12   Share Information

To answer these questions, visit the library or use a search engine on the Internet, such as Lycos, Yahoo, or AltaVista. As you write your answers, use sentence rearrangement and combining techniques. Your instructor will explain how to complete this section regarding the number of questions to answer and whether to work independently, with a partner, or in a group.

The Cowboy's Uniform

1. In addition to the cowboy's hat, what else does the cowboy wear? Explain the significance and value of each item.

2. What is a cattle trail drive? Describe the routine and trip.

3. What is a ranch? What is a dude ranch?

4. Who were the cattle barons?

5. Who is a cowgirl noted in history? For what is she known?

Blue Jeans—An American Classic

6. What was the Gold Rush of 1849?

7. How did miners pan for gold?

8. Why was San Francisco important during the mid-nineteenth century?

9. What were different styles of jeans during the twentieth century?

Thimble and Thread

10. How have men's collar styles varied since the American Revolution? Highlight a few examples.

11. How is sheep's fleece made into cloth?

12. How does the product of a cotton plant become cloth?

13. How are natural products used to dye cloth?

Apron—A Style for Every Need

14. What is a lead apron? What professions utilize lead aprons?

The Necktie—A Link to the Past

15. Who was King Louis XIV? Why was he called the "Sun King"?

16. What is a black tie event? A white tie event?

17. What is the correct way to tie a four-in-hand knot? Windsor? Half Windsor? Bow tie?

More About Attire

18. What are the parts of a spacesuit? Label a picture explaining the function of each part.

19. What are the parts of a fireman's suit? Label a picture explaining the function of each part.

20. What are the parts of a deep-sea diver's outfit? Label a picture explaining the function of each part.

21. What were the parts of medieval armor? Label a picture explaining the function of each part.

22. Who was Issac Singer? What was the significance of his invention?

EXERCISE 13   Understand Idioms

What is the meaning of each of the following idioms related to clothing? To find the meaning, check a dictionary or a specialized idiom dictionary, or ask someone who understands the idiom to explain it to you.

come to the end of one's rope

know the ropes

give one enough rope

give one the boot

just a thimbleful

hang by a thread

pull the wool over someone's eyes

dyed-in-the-wool

patch up a quarrel

tied to one's mother's apron strings

sew up a deal

CHAPTER 7

The Changing American Scene

A place belongs forever to whoever claims it hardest, remembers it most obsessively, wrenches it from itself, shapes it, renders it, loves it so radically that he remakes it in his own image.

— Joan Didion (b. 1934)

As time passes, memories of special places endure. In this chapter you will read about one place that is part of the American past: the drive-in movie theater.

Connecting Reading with Writing

EXERCISE 1   Reflections on the Changing American Scene

1.   What do you like about watching a movie in a movie theater?

_____

_____

_____

2.   What do you like about watching a movie at home?

_____

_____

_____

The American Drive-In Theater

1   In the early 1930s Richard Hollingshead placed a movie projector on the hood of his car, nailed a screen to the trees at the end of his driveway, and placed a radio behind the screen for sound. Hollingshead believed that spacious American cars would provide a comfortable private room from which to watch movies. He obtained a patent for a motion picture theater—the drive-in theater—and several years later, he built the world's first drive-in theater in Camden, New Jersey.

2   On June 6, 1933, the first customers at the Camden Drive-In Theater paid 25 cents per car and an additional 25 cents per person. These customers saw *Wife Beware,* a second-rate feature from 1932. From this simple start, thousands of drive-in theaters appeared across the United States by the 1950s. The drive-in theater was a place where people

were entertained in convenience and privacy while being part of a community.

3   The outdoor movie theater appealed to the American family's budget and sense of adventure. Home entertainment was limited to the radio and perhaps several channels on a small black-and-white television screen. Now, parents could pack kids, blankets, and pillows into the spacious back seat of their car and head off for a night of family fun. Once at the drive-in, the parents parked in their favorite spot and rolled down a window to hang a small speaker box. Before the first movie began, children raced off to play on slides, swings, seesaws, and merry-go-rounds. Some theaters offered pony rides, train rides, and even swimming pools.

4   Between 1946 and 1953, 2,976 drive-ins were built. By 1958, the number peaked at more than 4,000. Various slang nicknames for the drive-ins were "fresh-air exhibitors," "outdooers," "open air operators," "underskyers," and "ozoner."

5   By the mid-1950s, the drive-in became a popular hangout for teenagers who had extra pocket money and cars and wanted a place away from parents. The drive-in became the perfect social center to eat hot dogs and pizza, drink cherry sodas, and socialize. Romantic and exciting, the drive-ins attracted teenagers with low-budget films like *I Was a Teenage Werewolf* and *The Blob*. As more and more drive-in theaters catered to teenagers, the drive-ins became known as "passion pits."

6   A focal point of the drive-in theater was the enormous screen towers. The side of the screen tower facing the highway was painted with elaborate murals depicting community interests, such as cowboys, a huge steer, or a school's mascot. In order to attract passing motorists, the drive-in theaters decorated the murals with brilliantly colored neon lights. Because the drive-ins were very dark at night, drive-in owners installed tall muted lights, known as "moonglow" lights, to make sure patrons could get to the food concession stands not only before the show but also during the ten-minute intermission.

7   The drive-in movie theater all but vanished by the end of the 1960s. Its reputation as a passion pit, coupled with more television channel choices at home, drove away family audiences. Many drive-in theaters located at the edge of a town sold their property to shopping mall corporations. Other theaters, abandoned by owners who no longer could afford the upkeep, lay as dilapidated remnants of a time gone by.

8   By the close of the twentieth century, there were fewer than 900 functioning drive-ins. The drive-in movie theater, a uniquely American institution, is best remembered today as an icon of another era.

EXERCISE 2   Questions About the Reading

Select the letter that best completes each question or statement.

1. This passage focuses on discussing

    A. the brief popularity of the American drive-in.

    B. the popularity of the food concessions.

    C. the American drive-in as a teenage hangout.

    D. the benefits of drive-in entertainment.

2. Choose the sentence that tells the main idea.

    A. The drive-in was a hangout for rebellious teenagers.

    B. The drive-in promoted community spirit.

    C. The drive-in was a popular place to spend an inexpensive night out.

    D. The drive-in's large screen was an environmental concern during the 1950s.

3. Which of the following is *not* another name for drive-in?

    A. ozoners

    B. fresh air exhibitors

    C. passion pits

    D. outdoor babysitters

4. From this passage it is clear

    A. why the drive-in was a uniquely American institution.

    B. what typical drive-ins across the United States looked like.

    C. how local drive-ins encouraged community spirit.

    D. why the drive-in appealed to families and teenagers.

5. The author probably tells about "moonglow" lights

    A. to illustrate how dark it was at a drive-in theater.

    B. to describe the romantic environment of a drive-in theater.

    C. to explain how drive-in owners encouraged concession sales.

    D. to persuade readers to purchase similar lights.

6. As used in the sentence, "The drive-in movie theater, a uniquely American institution, is best remembered today as an *icon* of another era," the word *icon* means

   A. problem.

   B. symbol.

   C. ideal.

   D. tradition.

EXERCISE 3   Sentence Explication

1. Either use the sentence that follows, or select and copy a different sentence from the reading selection.

   By the mid-1950s, the drive-in became a popular hangout for teenagers who had extra pocket money and cars and wanted a place away from parents.

   paragraph #4

   Or the sentence you choose:

   _____

   _____

   paragraph #____

2. Paraphrase the sentence by rewriting it in your own words.

   _____

   _____

   _____

   _____

3. React to the sentence. What comments and questions do you have about it?

   _____

   _____

_____

_____

4. Relate to the sentence. What personal experiences does it bring to mind?

_____

_____

_____

_____

EXERCISE 4 Questions for Writing and Discussion

1. Why was the drive-in theater popular entertainment during the middle decades of the twentieth century?

2. What features of the drive-in theater's construction were effective marketing devices?

3. Why did the drive-in theater decline in popularity during the 1960s?

Working from Sentences to Paragraph

Rearrange Sentences with New Beginnings

A good name is better than riches.

— Miguel de Cervantes (1547–1616)

EXERCISE 5 The Tavern

Part A

Use the provided new sentence beginnings to change the emphasis of the following sentences that describe a place where people met to have a beer and to

socialize long before America became the United States. As you rearrange the words, be sure to keep the meaning of the original sentence.

1. The tavern was a popular social and political center in early American life.

    In early American life _____

    _____

    _____

2. People went to taverns to eat and drink, play a game of cards, discuss the news of the day, or drop off mail to a passing traveler.

    At the tavern, people ate _____

    _____

    _____

3. In Manhattan, one of the most popular taverns in the 1640s was The Tavern of the Wooden Horse.

    In the 1640s, _____

    _____

    _____

4. The tavern was given its famous name by the owner who endured a harsh punishment.

    The owner _____

    _____

    _____

5. He had been sentenced by the local authorities "to ride the wooden horse" because he was absent from military duty without leave.

   After being absent _____

   _____

   _____

6. The phrase "to ride the wooden horse" meant to sit on a sawhorse built with long legs.

   The meaning _____

   _____

   _____

7. With weights up to fifty pounds attached to each of his legs, the punished person sat astride[1] the wooden horse for hours on public display.

   For hours _____

   _____

   _____

8. To make clear he had been at work in his tavern instead of on duty, the tavern owner also had to hold a drawn sword in one hand and a pitcher of beer in the other.

   Holding _____

   _____

   _____

[1] **astride** with a leg on each side

9. He was punished for two hours a day for one week.

   His punishment _____

   _____

   _____

10. Soon after the tavern owner served his sentence, he resigned from the service.

    The tavern owner _____

    _____

    _____

11. Then he placed a freshly painted board outside his tavern telling its new name, The Tavern of the Wooden Horse.

    He painted _____

    _____

    _____

Part B

After checking your rearranged sentences with your instructor, copy them to create a paragraph.

*We are living in a world today where
lemonade is made from artificial flavors and
furniture polish is made from real lemons.*
— Alfred E. Newman (1900–1970)

Combine Sentences with New Beginnings

EXERCISE 6   The Soda Fountain

Part A

Read the following draft of a descriptive paragraph about a bygone spot, popular for socializing and sweet treats. In Parts B and C, you will work on combining sentences and adding transitions to make the paragraph coherent.

Years ago people enjoyed going to a soda fountain. A soda fountain served refreshments. A soda fountain was a place located in a pharmacy. Pharmacy windows had displays. The displays were elaborate. The displays attracted customers to the soda fountain. Customers sat on stools to get served. The stools were tall. The stools were next to a counter. The counter was made of marble or onyx. Large containers of carbonated water were installed in the counter. A row of silver-plated syrup pumps was inserted in the counter. This was typical. Soda fountains offered beverages. There were at least thirty different kinds of soda beverages. The server made ice cream sodas. He scooped ice cream into a tall glass. He squirted seltzer water into the tall glass. Sometimes he squirted syrup over ice cream. The syrup flavors were chocolate, strawberry, raspberry, or pineapple. This happned in the 1950s. Soda fountains became after-school hangouts. They were popular hangouts for teenagers. This is what teenagers would do at the soda fountains. They sipped their sodas. They read comic books. They listened to music. Most of all, they socialized.

Part B

Combine the ideas from the sentences in each group to write one new sentence. Begin the new sentence using the indicated words. As you write the sentence, think about the emphasis and relationships you want to achieve.

1.

Years ago people enjoyed going to a soda fountain.

A soda fountain served refreshments.

A soda fountain was a place located in a pharmacy.

Years ago _____

_____

_____

2.

Pharmacy windows had displays.

The displays were elaborate.

The displays attracted customers to the soda fountain.

Elaborate _____

_____

_____

3.

Customers sat on stools to get served.

The stools were tall.

The stools were next to a counter.

The counter was made of marble or onyx.

To get served _____

_____

_____

4.

Large containers of carbonated water were installed in the counter.

A row of silver-plated syrup pumps was installed in the counter.

In the counter _____

_____

_____

5.

This was typical.

Soda fountains offered beverages.

There were at least thirty different kinds of soda beverages.

Typically _____

_____

_____

6.

The server made ice cream sodas.

He scooped ice cream into a tall glass.

He squirted seltzer water into the tall glass.

To make _____

_____

_____

7.

Sometimes he squirted syrup over ice cream.

The syrup flavors were chocolate, strawberry, raspberry, or pineapple.

Over ice cream _____

_____

_____

8.

This happened in the 1950s.

Soda fountains became after-school hangouts.

They were popular hangouts for teenagers.

During the 1950s _____

_____

_____

9.

This is what teenagers would do at soda fountains.

They sipped their sodas.

They read comic books.

They listened to music.

Most of all, they socialized.

Teenagers went to _____

_____

_____

Part C

After checking your combined sentences with your instructor, copy them to create a paragraph. Add transitions to make the paragraph coherent. Note the differences between the original and the rewritten paragraphs.

Combine Sentences on Your Own

Those who don't read have no advantage
over those who can't.

— Mark Twain (1835–1910)

EXERCISE 7   The One-Room Schoolhouse

Part A

Read the following draft of a descriptive paragraph about the ancestor of the modern American school. In Parts B and C, you will work on combining sentences and adding transitions to make the paragraph coherent.

In the early days, children attended a one-room schoolhouse. As many as forty children attended a one-room schoolhouse. They were taught by one "school-marm." This was typical. The teacher was not much older than the oldest students she taught. The teacher had at least a high school education. Sometimes, school districts had a number of restrictions. These restrictions were placed on female teachers. A teacher was often forbidden to marry. She was forbidden to "keep company." She was forbidden to ride in a vehicle with any man but her father or brother. A teacher taught from spellers. Spellers contained lessons. These lessons included spelling, arithmetic, geography, and morality. A popular speller was *Webster's Elementary Spelling Book*. The popular speller was known as the blue-backed speller. Blue paper covered the wooden boards binding the book. There were no assistant teachers to help students. There were no aides to help students. Students learned how to help each other. Students learned how to help themselves.

Part B

Revise the paragraph by combining the ideas from the sentences in each group to write one new sentence. As you write each sentence, think about the emphasis and relationships you want to achieve, adding transitions as needed.

1.

In the early days, children attended a one-room schoolhouse.

As many as forty children attended a one-room schoolhouse.

They were taught by one "schoolmarm."

_____

_____

_____

_____

2.

This was typical.

The teacher was not much older than the oldest students she taught.

The teacher had at least a high school education.

_____

_____

_____

_____

3.

Sometimes, school districts had a number of restrictions.

These restrictions were placed on female teachers.

_____

_____

_____

_____

4.

A teacher was often forbidden to marry.

She was forbidden to "keep company."

She was forbidden to ride in a vehicle with any man but her father or brother.

_____

_____

_____

_____

5.

A teacher taught from spellers.

Spellers contained lessons.

These lessons included spelling, arithmetic, geography, and morality.

_____

_____

_____

_____

6.

A popular speller was *Webster's Elementary Spelling Book.*

The speller was known as the blue-backed speller.

Blue paper covered the wooden boards binding the book.

_____

_____

_____

_____

7.

There were no assistant teachers to help students.

There were no aides to help students.

Students learned how to help each other.

Students learned how to help themselves.

_____

_____

_____

_____

Part C

After you have checked your sentences with your instructor, copy them to create a coherent paragraph. Note the differences between the original and the rewritten paragraphs.

Identify Sentences in Context

A wise man can see more from the bottom of
a well than a fool can from a mountaintop.

— Anonymous

EXERCISE 8   The Outhouse

The following paragraph about the old-time privy is missing periods. Add a period to mark the end of a sentence and capitalize the beginning word of the next sentence. Copy on the adjacent numbered line each word you have capitalized.

Campers today may be some of the few people who are familiar with the outdoor toilet facility sometimes called a privy, necessarium, latrine, or comfort station, an outhouse was at one time a common sight easy to build, an outhouse was nothing more than a wooden shed with a roof, a floor, and a front door the average outhouse was four-by-four feet square and seven feet high in the outhouse was a box about two feet high and two feet deep built along the back wall an oblong shape was cut on top of the box the outhouse was set over a hole dug about five feet into the ground it was common to use a circular symbol representing the sun on the door to identify the men's facility and a quarter-moon on the door to identify the women's these universal signs, especially common at inns and boarding houses, were helpful for people

1. _____
2. _____
3. _____
4. _____
5. _____
6. _____
7. _____
8. _____
9. _____
10. _____
11. _____
12. _____
13. _____
14. _____
15. _____
16. _____

who were illiterate or who were traveling from non-English speaking countries the development of efficient water and sewage systems and the invention of the "water closet" replaced the outhouse most people were not unhappy to see this building pass from the American scene.	17. _____ 18. _____ 19. _____ 20. _____ 21. _____ 22. _____

Rearrange and Combine Sentences Using Transitions

No one likes to be the first to step on the ice.

— Yugoslavian proverb

EXERCISE 9   The Icehouse

Part A

Read a draft of an informative paragraph about a cool house where no one lived. In Parts B and C, you will work on combining, rearranging, and adding transitions to make the paragraph coherent.

Until well into the twentieth century, families used natural ice for cooling food. Natural ice was stored in icehouses. Icehouses were made of rough lumber insulated with sawdust. Icehouses were located next to a stream or pond. Workers cut and stored natural ice during January, February, and March. Harvesting ice in bitter cold was hard work. The work took from dawn to dusk. Workers cut ice into sheets with ice plows. Workers separated the sheets into cakes. Workers packed the ice with space between the layers. The space allowed for melting and prevented the cakes from freezing into one solid block. The ice in the icehouse lasted until into August. Families used the ice from the icehouse for their iceboxes. An icebox was a wooden box inside the house for keeping foods cold.

Part B

Revise the paragraph by using rearrangement, combining, and transitions *wherever appropriate* to create new sentences. Not every sentence needs to be rewritten.

1. Until well into the twentieth century, families used natural ice for cooling food.

2. Natural ice was stored in icehouses.

3. Icehouses were made of rough lumber insulated with sawdust.

4. Icehouses were located next to a stream or pond.

5. Harvesting ice in bitter cold was hard work.

6. The work took from dawn to dusk.

7. Workers cut and stored natural ice during January, February, and March.

8. Workers cut ice into sheets with an ice plow.

9. Workers separated the sheets into cakes.

10. Workers packed the cakes with space between the layers.

11. The space allowed for melting and prevented the cakes from freezing into one solid block.

12. The ice in the ice house lasted until August.

13. Families used the ice for their iceboxes.

14. An icebox was a wooden box inside the house for keeping foods cold.

Part C

After you have checked your sentences with your instructor, copy them to create a paragraph. Note the differences between the original and the rewritten paragraphs.

Writing from Experience

EXERCISE 10   Write a Paragraph

Write a paragraph of 8–12 sentences on one of the following topics.

1. Some older adults today remember with fondness the time they spent at the local drug store soda fountain. Describe a place that brings you positive memories—at home, at school, in the community.

   Questions to Consider

   What is the place and where is it located?

   What details about the place are important?

   How recently have you visited the place?

   What memories do you have about being in this place?

2. Students in a traditional one-room schoolhouse usually had a young female teacher to help them learn their lessons. They might have had this same teacher year after year as they moved up through the grades. Chances are you have had many teachers during your own school days. Write about one of your teachers.

   Questions to Consider

   What subject and grade did the teacher teach you?

   What do you remember most about the teacher?

   What experience or experiences do you remember?

   How did the teacher impact the way you felt about learning?

   Why would or wouldn't you recommend this teacher for someone else?

3. A favorite pastime of many people is to collect memorabilia, such as bottles, coins, trains, baseball cards, postcards, or records. Write about a collection belonging to you or someone you know.

   Questions to Consider

   What is the collection?

   When did the collection begin?

Why did the collection begin?

How did the collection begin?

Describe one or more of the most valued pieces of the collection.

What is the collector's feeling or attitude about the collection?

4. Like the soda fountain server, many people today have jobs serving others. These jobs may be in restaurants, stores, hospitals, and other places. Not only do these workers perform important functions, they also have an opportunity to learn from their work. Tell about what you have learned as a service employee.

Questions to Consider

In what job have you had a learning experience?

How long did you work (or have you worked) at this job?

What have you learned about the work, other people, and yourself?

How has this job influenced your career goals?

For question 5, you are on your own to create questions for development.

5. During the 1950s young people socialized at soda fountains and drive-ins. Today people also have places to go to spend leisure time with other people. Tell about a place where you enjoyed socializing when you were younger or a place that you enjoy today.

Questions for Development

_____

_____

_____

_____

_____

For question 6, you are on your own to decide a focus and to create questions for development.

6. Write on a topic of your choice about change.

Focus

_____

Questions for Development

_____

_____

_____

_____

_____

EXERCISE 11 Revise Your Paragraph

Part A
Reread the paragraph you wrote for Exercise 10.

1. Choose one sentence to rearrange.

    Original Sentence _____

    _____

    Rearranged Sentence _____

    _____

2. Choose two or more sentences that could be effectively combined.

    Original Sentences

    _____

    _____

_____

_____

Combined Sentences

_____

_____

_____

You may want to use these revised sentences in the final draft of your paragraph.

Part B
Check your paragraph before submitting your final draft.

A CLEAR TOPIC SENTENCE

❐   Does the topic sentence state the topic?

❐   Does the topic sentence state what you will tell about the topic?

CONVINCING SUPPORT

❐   Do your sentences say what you want them to mean?

❐   Have you included enough details to make your ideas clear?

EFFECTIVE ORGANIZATION

❐   Does the paragraph have a beginning, a middle, and an end?

❐   Does your concluding sentence provide a summary of your main idea?

❐   Do you use transitions to link your ideas?

SUCCESSFUL SENTENCES

❐   Is each sentence complete?

❐   Have you eliminated run-ons and fragments?

❐   Have you written each word you need?

❐   Have you used a spell checker, speller, or dictionary to be sure words are spelled correctly?

❐   Have you used the correct forms of homonyms?

EFFECTIVE TITLE

❏   Does your title suggest what the paragraph is about and make someone interested in reading it?

Writing from Resources

EXERCISE 12   Share Information

To answer these questions, visit the library or use a search engine on the Internet, such as Lycos, Yahoo, or AltaVista. As you write your answers, use sentence rearrangement and combining techniques. Your instructor will explain how to complete this section regarding the number of questions to answer and whether to work independently, with a partner, or in a group.

The Tavern

1.   Where is a restored tavern located? What is its history? What is significant about its name?

2.   How is beer made?

3.   In addition to riding the wooden horse, what other public punishments were practiced in colonial America?

4.   What is the role of state militia today?

The Soda Fountain

5.   What did a soda fountain look like? Describe the interior.

6.   What is a pharmacist? What are the educational requirements for today's pharmacist?

7.   What are the differences among the following types of water: carbonated water, hot mineral water, sparkling mineral water, seltzer water, filtered water?

The One-Room Schoolhouse

8. What was the typical training for teaching in a one-room schoolhouse?

9. What are the current qualifications required for teaching certification in your state?

10. What supplies were standard in a one-room schoolhouse?

11. What are the features of a one-room schoolhouse that has been preserved as a historic site. If possible, obtain pictures.

The Outhouse

12. What were the contributions of architect Isaiah Rogers to the Tremont Hotel in Boston? The Astor House in New York City?

13. What are international signs? Give some examples.

The Icehouse

14. What is the history of ice cream?

15. What is ice carving?

16. How is an igloo constructed?

More About the Changing American Scene

17. What building has been preserved in your community or state? What does it look like? What is its significance?

18. Places that were popular or in vogue at one time have either changed or are no longer part of the American scene. Choose one of the places and answer the following questions about it: What were its features? Why was it popular?

   gasoline service station

   Pullman sleeping car

   lighthouse

   general store

apothecary

barber shop

drive-in restaurant

EXERCISE 13   Understand Idioms

What is the meaning of each of the following idioms related to Americana? To find the meaning, check a dictionary or a specialized idiom dictionary, or ask someone who understands the idiom to explain it to you.

rule with an iron fist

hard and fast rule

tell tales out of school

read between the lines

wipe the slate clean

rule of thumb

teacher's pet

blackboard jungle

the golden rule

mind your manners

dunce cap

hickory stick

head of the class

straight answer

People working in a soda fountain used the following expressions. What do they mean?

soda jerk

bucket of mud

no cow

cold bag

sun-kissed

nervous pudding

fish eggs

rabbit food

sand and yum-yum

slice of squeal

stack

choker holes

sea dust

CHAPTER 8

American Folktales

Myth is an attempt to narrate a whole human experience, of which the purpose is too deep, going too deep in the blood and soul, for mental explanation or description.

— D. H. Lawrence (1885–1930)

Americans, like all peoples, have a wealth of stories to explain what they value and who they are. The reading in this chapter is about stories that have been told from generation to generation.

Connecting Reading with Writing

EXERCISE 1 Reflections on American Folktales

1. What information do people today learn by "word of mouth," in other words, by hearing it?

_____

_____

_____

2. What are the advantages and disadvantages of passing on information orally?

_____

_____

_____

Enjoying the World's Folktales

by Joanna Cole

1   Folktales and fairy tales are usually the first stories we hear as children, and almost no others can equal their power to involve us so totally. When Little Red Riding Hood says to the wolf, "What big eyes you have, Grandmother," the young child, listening with wide eyes herself, gives a shiver of delight tinged with fear. When Jack wakes to find that the worthless beans of yesterday have grown into a magic beanstalk, every child is as eager as Jack to find out what is at the top.

2   Although the tales are especially loved by children, the familiar nursery stories form only a small portion of the world's tales, most of which were not originally intended for children alone. In past times, folktales were told

in family or village groups, some stories told mainly to children, some to mixed groups, and some only to the adults of the community.

3   Because they are the products of preliterate societies, the folktales, unlike our modern novels and short stories, were not invented by a single author and printed in a book to be read unchanged forever. Instead, they were passed by word of mouth from one teller to another, never told twice in exactly the same way. This oral tradition made for a unique intimacy between teller and listeners, and the give-and-take with the audience no doubt influenced the form of the tales. Thus the stories express the wishes, hopes, and fears of many people, rather than the concerns of a particular writer, and they deal with universal human dilemmas that span differences of age, culture, and geography.

4   When heard again and again throughout a lifetime, the tales served not only to entertain but also to transmit the values and wisdom of the culture. They imbue[1] a strong sense of right and wrong and provide a reservoir of vivid images that became part of the individual's imagination and even of his everyday language.

5   The work the Brothers Grimm did to collect fairy tales in Germany had a profound[2] influence on the rest of Europe. Not only was their collection widely translated, but scholars in other countries began to follow their lead and collect the folktales of their own nations. It was not long before almost every European country had a folklore society, dedicated to preserving not only folktales but other folk literature as well: songs, poems, games, proverbs, folk remedies, weatherlore, and so on. After a time, the science of folklore spread to Asia, Africa, and the Americas, so that at present, tales have been published from almost everywhere.

6   As the tales accumulated, something amazing began to emerge: despite the cultural variation one would naturally expect in stories from different places, there were uncanny[3] similarities in tales from countries as far away from each other as India and Ireland. For instance, there are so many versions of the Cinderella story in the world that in 1893 a book was published that analyzed no fewer than 345 of them. Most of the other major folktale themes as well are told in hundreds of versions from one country to another.

7   To account for the existence of similar stories everywhere, some scholars believed that the world's tales originally spread from one source by

[1] **imbue**   instill, inspire, introduce

[2] **profound**   deep, weighty

[3] **uncanny**   surprising, extraordinary

8   diffusion.[4] That is, the plots were thought to have originated in India and traveled via pilgrims, merchants, and immigrants to local storytellers elsewhere, who adopted the stories as their own, changing details in the telling, but keeping the bones of the tales intact.[5]

9   Another theory was that the stories sprang up simultaneously in different countries because the material of the folktales is universal.[6] The themes were said to be those concerning human beings everywhere, and the stories were bound to be invented wherever communities developed.

Today most folklorists hold a kind of combination view; that is, some themes do seem to be universal, and stories centering on these arise independently in different places. Other specific plots have spread from a variety of places by diffusion.

EXERCISE 2   Questions About the Reading

Select the letter that best completes each question or statement.

1. The passage is mostly about folktales and

    A.   their common themes.

    B.   their history.

    C.   the Brothers Grimm.

    D.   their importance to children.

2. Choose the sentence that most clearly tells the main idea.

    A.   As the tales accumulated, something amazing began to emerge: despite the cultural variation one would naturally expect in stories from different places, there were uncanny similarities in tales from countries as far away from each other as India and Ireland.

    B.   This oral tradition made for a unique intimacy between teller and listeners, and the give-and-take with the audience no doubt influenced the form of the tales.

    C.   The stories express the wishes, hopes, and fears of many people, rather than the concerns of a particular writer, and they deal with universal human dilemmas that span differences of age, culture, and geography.

---

[4] **diffusion**   distribution, circulation

[5] **intact**   whole, in one piece

[6] **universal**   common, worldwide

D. Most of the major folktale themes are told in hundreds of versions from one country to another.

3. Which of the following is not mentioned in this passage as a role of folktales?

   A. The tales provide amusement.

   B. The tales teach about history.

   C. The tales illustrate right and wrong.

   D. The tales add vocabulary to a language.

4. The author suggests that folktales

   A. provide an understanding of a culture.

   B. were written mainly for children.

   C. have differing themes depending on their origin.

   D. are difficult to collect because they are oral.

5. This passage was written in order to

   A. describe collecting folktales.

   B. convince readers to read a variety of folktales.

   C. explain the universal appeal of folktales.

   D. entertain readers with folktales.

6. As used in the sentence ". . . the stories deal with universal human *dilemmas* that span differences of age, culture, and geography," *dilemmas* means

   A. populations.

   B. experiences.

   C. knowledge.

   D. problems.

EXERCISE 3   Sentence Explication

1. Either use the sentence that follows, or select and copy a different sentence from the reading selection.

   Folktales and fairy tales are usually the first stories we hear as children, and almost no others can equal their power to involve us so totally.

   paragraph #1

Or the sentence you choose:

_____

_____

paragraph #___

2. Paraphrase the sentence by rewriting it in your own words.

_____

_____

_____

_____

3. React to the sentence. What comments and questions do you have about it?

_____

_____

_____

_____

4. Relate to the sentence. What personal experiences does it bring to mind?

_____

_____

_____

_____

_____

EXERCISE 4   Questions for Writing and Discussion

1. How does the fact that folktales were originally told rather than written make them different from other stories?

2. Of what value were folktales to a community?

3. Why was the work of the Brothers Grimm important?

4. What theories explain the existence of similar stories in different cultures?

Working from Sentences to Paragraph

Rearrange Sentences with New Beginnings

Strength does not come from physical capacity.
It comes from an indomitable will.

— Mahatma Gandhi (1869–1948)

EXERCISE 5 Paul Bunyan

Part A

Use the provided new sentence beginnings to change the emphasis of the following sentences that tell about the proverbial American strongman with a kind heart, a mountain man as big as the whole outdoors. As you rearrange the words, be sure to keep the meaning of the original sentence.

1. Paul Bunyan's mother used a lumber wagon for her big child's baby carriage and some wheelbarrow wheels for buttons on his baby jacket.

   When Paul Bunyan _____

   _____

   _____

2. A frail blue ox swept on the ocean shore by an enormous white wave was found by Paul when he was grown.

Paul _____

_____

_____

3. Naming the ox Babe, he nursed it back to health with moose-moss soup.

He named the ox _____

_____

_____

4. Babe became powerful; he could bellow, paw, and snort like an ox ten times his size.

Babe bellowed _____

_____

_____

5. As a team, Paul cut down trees, and Babe dragged whole forests for the loggers.

Paul and Babe _____

_____

_____

6. Babe pulled the cookhouse, the bunkhouses, and all the other buildings on sleds behind him to help the loggers move from one state to another.

When the loggers _____

_____

_____

7. John Shears wanted to get rid of Babe, and he decided one day to poison the ox by feeding him a huge pile of poisoned parsnips.

John Shears, who _____

_____

_____

8. Little Meery, Paul's friend, saw a chance to save Babe by opening the beehive so the bees could swarm to the parsnips.

To save _____

_____

_____

9. The bees made a beeline for the parsnips and scared Babe away.

By making a beeline _____

_____

_____

10. John Shears was kicked so high by Babe he was not seen for three weeks.

Babe kicked _____

_____

_____

11. Little Meery was rewarded by Paul with an invitation to become one of Paul's loggers.

Paul rewarded _____

_____

_____

12. Big Paul Bunyan and his mighty blue ox Babe will be remembered in logging camps as long as loggers fell trees.

As long as _____

_____

_____

Part B

After checking your rearranged sentences with your instructor, copy them to create a paragraph.

Combine Sentences with New Beginnings

You can't run away from trouble. There ain't no place that far.

— Joel Chandler Harris (1848–1908)

EXERCISE 6   Getting the Last Laugh

Part A

Read the following draft of a narrative paragraph illustrating a folktale in the African-American tradition. In this story, like many others, the hero, a trickster, gets out of a difficult situation by fooling the villain. In Parts B and C, you will work on combining sentences and adding transitions to make the paragraph coherent.

Brer[1] Fox captured Brer Rabbit. Brer Fox yelled that Brer Rabbit had been sassy for too long. Brer Fox yelled that Brer Rabbit was constantly where he had no business being. The fox said that he would make a brush fire. He would barbecue the rabbit for dinner. Brer Rabbit had a plan that would fool the fox. He asked the fox not to throw him into the nearby briar patch.[2] The fox thought for a

[1] **Brer**   Brother
[2] **Briar patch**   clump of thorny bushes

moment. He said that he couldn't proceed with the barbecue. He said he had no string to tie Brer Rabbit to the spit. He decided to drown the rabbit instead. He quickly realized drowning wouldn't work. The water wasn't high enough. The fox had another plan. He would try to skin the rabbit. Brer Rabbit pleaded again with the fox. Skin me. Snatch out my eyeballs. Pull out my ears by the roots. Cut off my legs. Do any of these things. Don't throw me into the briar patch. The rabbit didn't want to be thrown into the briar patch. Brer Fox would do exactly what the rabbit didn't want him to do. The fox picked the rabbit up by the legs. The fox flung him into the briar patch. The fox waited to see what happened. Brer Fox could see Brer Rabbit. Brer Rabbit was up on the hill. Brer Rabbit was sitting cross-legged on a log. The rabbit sang. "Thank you, Brer Fox. I was born and bred in a briar patch." The rabbit skipped away. He was as lively as a cricket in the embers.

Part B

Combine the ideas from the sentences in each group to write one new sentence. Begin the new sentence using the indicated words. As you write the sentence, think about the emphasis and relationships you want to achieve.

1.

Brer Fox captured Brer Rabbit.

Brer Fox yelled that Brer Rabbit had been sassy for too long.

Brer Fox yelled that Brer Rabbit was constantly where he had no business being.

Brer Fox _____

_____

_____

_____

_____

2.

The fox said that he would make a brush fire.

He would barbecue the rabbit for dinner.

The fox _____

_____

_____

_____

_____

3.

Brer Rabbit had a plan that would fool the fox.

He asked the fox not to throw him into the nearby briar patch.

With a plan _____

_____

_____

_____

4.

The fox thought for a moment.

He said that he couldn't proceed with the barbecue.

He said he had no string to tie Brer Rabbit to the pit.

The fox, after thinking _____

_____

_____

_____

5.

He decided to drown the rabbit instead.

He realized drowning wouldn't work.

The water wasn't high enough.

Instead _____

_____

_____

_____

_____

6.

The fox had another plan.

He would try to skin the rabbit.

Another plan _____

_____

_____

_____

_____

7.

Brer Rabbit pleaded again with the fox.

Skin me.

Snatch out my eyeballs.

Pull out my ears by the roots.

Cut off my legs.

Do any of these things.

Don't throw me into the briar patch.

Pleading with the fox, Brer Rabbit said _____

_____

_____

_____

_____

8.

The rabbit didn't want to be thrown into the briar patch.

Brer Fox would do exactly what the rabbit didn't want him to do.

Since the rabbit _____

_____

_____

_____

9.

The fox picked the rabbit up by the legs.

The fox flung him into the briar patch.

The fox waited to see what happened.

Picking the rabbit up by the legs _____

_____

_____

_____

_____

10.

Brer Fox could see Brer Rabbit.

Brer Rabbit was up on the hill.

Brer Rabbit was sitting cross-legged on a log.

Soon Brer Fox could see _____

_____

_____

_____

11.

The rabbit sang.

"Thank you, Brer Fox. I was born and bred in a briar patch."

The rabbit skipped away.

He was as lively as a cricket in the embers.

"Thank you, Brer Fox. I was born and bred in a briar patch," _____

_____

_____

_____

Part C

After checking your combined sentences with your instructor, copy them to create a paragraph. Add transitions and linking words to make the paragraph coherent. Note the differences between the original and the rewritten paragraphs.

Combine Sentences on Your Own

Five enemies of peace inhabit with us—
avarice, ambition, envy, anger, and pride;
if these were to be banished, we should
infallibly enjoy perpetual peace.

— Francesco Petrarch (1304–1374)

EXERCISE 7   **Pride Comes Before a Fall**

Part A

Read the following draft of a narrative paragraph that retells a tale from Native American lore. In this tradition, an animal often illustrates a truth about human nature. In Parts B and C, you will work on combining sentences and adding transitions to make the paragraph coherent.

The rooster was the most boastful animal in the village. He said he would be the head dancer at the powwow dance. The dance started. The rooster was the first to head for the center of the dance grounds. The rooster swung to and fro. He danced close to the fire so he could be easily seen. His tall, draping tail feathers got too close to the fire. They began to smoke. They began to flame. Rooster saw the other dancers stop to point at him. Rooster thought they were admiring his footwork. Rooster thought they were admiring his style. He stuck out his chest even bigger. He partially closed his eyes. He pushed his head back and forth. He raised his beak high in the air. The rooster smelled a peculiar odor. He looked back. He was shocked to see his beautiful tail feathers on fire. He let out a shriek. The shriek echoed through the forests. The shriek echoed up the sides of the mountains. The rooster flapped his wings to put out the flames. The flapping caused his tail feathers to burn even more. He flew off into the night. He rose higher and higher into the sky. He was out of sight. Some say they see a blazing object in the sky at night. The object roams the sky with a fiery tail behind it. Some call the blazing object a comet. Others know it is just the rooster. The rooster is still trying to put out the flames in his tail feathers.

Part B

Revise the paragraph by combining the ideas from the sentences in each group to write one new sentence. As you write each sentence, think about the emphasis and relationships you want to achieve, adding transitions as needed.

1.

The rooster was the most boastful animal in the village.

He said he would be the head dancer at the powwow dance.

_____

_____

_____

_____

2.

The dance started.

The rooster was the first to head for the center of the dance grounds.

_____

_____

_____

_____

3.

The rooster swung to and fro.

He danced close to the fire so he could be easily seen.

_____

_____

_____

_____

4.

His tall, draping tail feathers got too close to the fire.

They began to smoke.

They began to flame.

_____

_____

_____

_____

5.

Rooster saw the other dancers stop to point at him.

Rooster thought they were admiring his footwork.

Rooster thought they were admiring his style.

_____

_____

_____

_____

6.

He stuck out his chest even bigger.

He partially closed his eyes.

He pushed his head back and forth.

He raised his beak high in the air.

_____

_____

_____

_____

7.

The rooster smelled a peculiar odor.

He looked back.

He was shocked to see his beautiful tail feathers on fire.

_____

_____

_____

_____

8.

He let out a shriek.

The shriek echoed through the forests.

The shriek echoed up the sides of the mountains.

_____

_____

_____

_____

9.

The rooster flapped his wings to put out the flames.

The flapping caused his tail feathers to burn even more.

_____

_____

_____

_____

10.

He flew off into the night.

He rose higher and higher into the sky.

He was out of sight.

_____

_____

_____

_____

11.

Some say they see a blazing object in the sky at night.

The object roams the sky with a fiery tail behind it.

_____

_____

_____

_____

12.

Some call this blazing object a comet.

Others know it is just the rooster.

The rooster is still trying to put out the flames in his tail feathers.

_____

_____

_____

_____

Part C

After you have checked your sentences with your instructor, copy them to create a coherent paragraph. Note the differences between the original and the rewritten paragraphs.

Identify Sentences in Context

I float like a butterfly, sting like bee.
— Muhammad Ali (b. 1942)

EXERCISE 8   Skinning a Bear: A Tall Tale About a Strong Woman

The following paragraph that retells a legend about an unbelievably fearless superwoman is missing periods. Add a period to mark the end of a sentence and capitalize the beginning word of the next sentence. Copy on the adjacent numbered line each word you have capitalized.

This story about Melinda Sue, a woman of the mountains, is based mostly on what some people believe to be facts the story says that one day, when Melinda Sue was going to a quilting bee with her lunch under her arm, she saw a big bear coming out of a hollow tree the bear looked at her and then at her lunch as if he didn't know what to eat first he poked out his nose and smelled the lunch of sausages made of rabbit meat and crocodile liver looking at him, Melinda Sue stood still for a minute in hopes he would feel ashamed of himself and go off when the bear began to smell her, she knew it was time to be stirring she tossed her dinner down before him as he put his nose to it to take a bite, she threw herself on him, catching

1. _____
2. _____
3. _____
4. _____
5. _____
6. _____
7. _____
8. _____
9. _____
10. _____
11. _____
12. _____
13. _____
14. _____

the scuff of his neck in her teeth he tried to run, but
she held on with her teeth that were long and sharp as
nails she stripped the skin clear off that bear, leaving
him as naked as he was the day he was born a week
afterwards the bear was seen running without his skin
up in Otter Clearing Melinda Sue made herself a
good warm petticoat out of the pesky varmint's hide
not surprisingly, she was never bothered by any bear
again as long as she lived in those mountains.

15. _____

16. _____

17. _____

18. _____

19. _____

20. _____

21. _____

22. _____

23. _____

Rearrange and Combine Sentences Using Transitions

*We really are 15 countries, and it's really
remarkable that each of us thinks we represent
the real America. The Midwesterner in Kansas,
the black American in Durham—both are
certain they are the real American.*

— Maya Angelou (b. 1928)

EXERCISE 9   Uncle Sam: U.S. Champion

Part A

Read a draft of an informative paragraph explaining the origins of a figure used to represent the United States. In Parts B and C, you will work on combining, rearranging, and adding transitions to make the paragraph coherent.

The events happened during the War of 1812. The legend grew out of Troy, New York. Sam Wilson was a meat packer. Sam Wilson packed meat in barrels. The barrels were shipped to soldiers. The barrels were stamped "US." The "US" meant United States. The soldiers said the meat came from their "Uncle Sam." The soldiers were joking. Word spread about Uncle Sam. Editorial cartoonists created a character. The name of the character was Uncle Sam. Uncle Sam represented the United States. Uncle Sam was a tall man. Uncle Sam was thin. Uncle Sam had a white beard. Uncle Sam wore a top hat. Uncle Sam wore a blue coat. Uncle Sam wore red and white striped pants. Drawings of Uncle Sam appeared on posters. The posters were used to recruit for the armed services.

Part B

Revise the paragraph by using rearrangement, combining, and transitions *wherever appropriate* to create new sentences. Not every sentence needs to be rewritten.

1. The events happened during the War of 1812.

2. The legend grew out of Troy, New York.

3. Sam Wilson was a meat packer.

4. Sam Wilson packed meat in barrels.

5. The barrels were shipped to soldiers

6. The barrels were stamped "US."

7. The "US" meant United States.

8. The soldiers said the meat came from their "Uncle Sam."

9. The soldiers were joking.

10. Word spread about Uncle Sam.

11. Editorial cartoonists created a character.

12. The name of the character was Uncle Sam.

13. Uncle Sam represented the United States.

14. Uncle Sam was a tall man.

15. Uncle Sam was thin.

16. Uncle Sam had a white beard.

17. Uncle Sam wore a top hat.

18. Uncle Sam wore a blue coat.

19. Uncle Sam wore red and white striped pants.

20. Drawings of Uncle Sam appeared on posters

21. The posters were used to recruit for the armed services.

Part C

After you have checked your sentences with your instructor, copy them to create a paragraph. Note the differences between the original and the rewritten paragraphs.

Writing from Experience

EXERCISE 10   Write a Paragraph

Write a paragraph of 8–12 sentences on one of the following topics:

1. Paul Bunyan, like many folk heroes, is too extraordinary to be believed. Create your own unbelievably strong, smart, powerful, or otherwise superior hero. Write a story involving this character.

   Questions to Consider

   Who is the hero? What is special about him/her?

   Where does this story take place? When does it take place?

   What happens from beginning to end?

   What does somebody learn or realize from the episode?

2. Brer Fox wanted to get the best of Brer Rabbit, but Brer Rabbit had the last laugh. Think about a situation in which you played a practical joke on someone else or had a joke played on you. Maybe someone tried to trick you in other ways. The trick may have been playful or serious. Explain the results of the practical joke or trick.

    Questions to Consider

    What was the trick?

    Who was involved in the trick?

    Where were you when the trick happened?

    When did the trick happen?

    How did you feel about the trick?

3. Babe, the Blue Ox; Brer Fox and Brer Rabbit; and the Rooster in the tales in this chapter all show human characteristics. Your pet or another animal you know may also seem like a person in some ways. Describe how an animal you know acts human.

    Questions to Consider

    What pet are you discussing?

    What does this pet look like?

    What does the pet do that seems human?

    How do people react to the pet?

4. Perhaps your family has stories that you tell and retell when members of the family are together. Relate one of the stories.

    Questions to Consider

    What is the story about?

    Who usually tells the story?

    What is the story?

    How do family members react?

For question 5, you are on your own to create questions for development.

5. In the tall tale "Skinning a Bear," Melinda Sue shows unbelievable strength in reacting to a difficult situation. People leading everyday lives, too, often react with strength in an emergency or during a trying time. This strength may be physical, mental, and/or emotional. Tell about a time that you or someone you know demonstrated strength.

    Questions for Development

    _____

    _____

    _____

    _____

    _____

    _____

For question 6, you are on your own to decide a focus and to create questions for development.

6. Write on a topic suggested by this chapter.

    Focus

    _____

    Questions for Development

    _____

    _____

    _____

    _____

EXERCISE 11   Revise Your Paragraph

Part A
Reread the paragraph you wrote for Exercise 10.

1. Choose one sentence to rearrange.

   Original Sentence _____

   _____

   Rearranged Sentence _____

   _____

2. Choose two or more sentences that could be effectively combined.

   Original Sentences

   _____

   _____

   _____

   _____

   Combined Sentences

   _____

   _____

   _____

You may want to use these revised sentences in the final draft of your paragraph.

Part B
Check your paragraph before submitting your final draft.

A CLEAR TOPIC SENTENCE

❑   Does the topic sentence state the topic?

❑   Does the topic sentence state what you will tell about the topic?

CONVINCING SUPPORT

❒ Do your sentences say what you want them to mean?

❒ Have you included enough details to make your ideas clear?

EFFECTIVE ORGANIZATION

❒ Does the paragraph have a beginning, a middle, and an end?

❒ Does your concluding sentence provide a summary of your main idea?

❒ Do you use transitions to link your ideas?

SUCCESSFUL SENTENCES

❒ Is each sentence complete?

❒ Have you eliminated run-ons and fragments?

❒ Have you written each word you need?

❒ Have you used a spell checker, speller, or dictionary to be sure words are spelled correctly?

❒ Have you used the correct form of homonyms?

EFFECTIVE TITLE

❒ Does your title suggest what the paragraph is about and make someone interested in reading it?

Writing from Resources

EXERCISE 12   Share Information

To answer these questions, visit the library or use a search engine on the Internet, such as Lycos, Yahoo, or AltaVista. As you write your answers, use sentence rearrangement and combining techniques.

Your instructor will explain how to complete this section regarding the number of questions to answer and whether to work independently, with a partner, or in a group.

Paul Bunyan

1. Where are statues of Paul Bunyan, his girlfriend, and blue ox Babe located? Describe these folk heroes.

2. What is the job of today's logger? What is a forester?

3. What is reforestation? Why is it important?

4. What are parsnips? What is their value? What is a recipe for using them?

5. What are other tales about Paul Bunyan?

Getting the Last Laugh

6. Who is Joel Chandler Harris? What did he write about?

7. What have reviewers over the years said about the Uncle Remus stories?

8. Who is Aesop? What do Harris and Aesop have in common?

9. Who is Bugs Bunny? What are his characteristics? What do Brer Rabbit and Bugs Bunny have in common?

Pride Comes Before a Fall

10. What is a Native American powwow? What is the importance of the drum? Music? Costumes?

11. What is a comet? When should a comet next be visible?

Skinning a Bear: A Tall Tale About a Strong Woman

12. What is a quilting bee? Why were they popular during past centuries? What similar activities, if any, take place today?

13. How can bears be a nuisance at the national parks? In what ways are people to blame?

14. What is a taxidermist? In what ways is taxidermy an art?

Uncle Sam: U.S. Champion

15. What characteristics of legendary figure Uncle Sam made him a national figure? Find pictures of him as he has evolved over the years.

16. What are the physical characteristics of the bald eagle? In what ways is the bald eagle a suitable national symbol?

17. When was the United States flag adopted? Who designed it? How has the appearance of the flag changed over the years?

18. What are military rations? How have they changed over the years?

More About American Folktales

19. Find a legend or tale not included in this chapter. What is the title of the story? Where did the story originate? What happens in the story? What lesson about human behavior does the story provide?

EXERCISE 13   Understand Idioms

What is the meaning of each of the following idioms related to American folktales? To find the meaning, check a dictionary or a specialized idiom dictionary, or ask someone who understands the idiom to explain it to you.

old fox

'til the cows come home

pull a rabbit out of the hat

in fine fettle

once in a blue moon

Mother Earth

fancy footwork

turned tail and ran

puffed up with pride

thereby hangs a tale

beat around the bush

rule the roost

CHAPTER 9

The American Outdoors

Speak to the earth and it shall teach thee.

— Job 12:8

The lands of America, reaching from the semitropics to the arctic, provide a wonderment of treasures to those who seek them. The reading in this chapter reveals how Native Americans viewed the land. Seattle, chief of the Squamish Indians, wrote to the American government in the 1850s. Although there is some question as to whether the following letter is an exact replication of Chief Seattle's 1854 letter to President Franklin Pierce, the message is worth considering even today, a century and a half after it was written.

Connecting Reading with Writing

EXERCISE 1   Reflections on the American Outdoors

1. Why do many people enjoy being outdoors?

    _____

    _____

    _____

2. What measures have been taken to preserve America's natural resources?

    _____

    _____

    _____

Chief Seattle's Letter

1   The president in Washington sends word that he wishes to buy our land. But how can you buy or sell the sky? The land? The idea is strange to us. If we do not own the freshness of the air and the sparkle of the water, how can you buy them?

2   Every part of the earth is sacred to my people. Every shining pine needle, every sandy shore, every mist in the dark woods, every meadow, every humming insect. All are holy in the memory and experience of my people.

3   We know the sap that courses through the trees as we know the blood that courses through our veins. We are part of the earth and it is part of us.

The perfumed flowers are our sisters. The bear, the deer, the great eagle, these are our brothers. The rocky crests, the dew in the meadow, the body heat of the pony, and man all belong to the same family.

4   The shining water that moves in the streams and rivers is not just water, but the blood of our ancestors. If we sell you our land, you must remember that it is sacred. Each glossy reflection in the clear waters of the lakes tells of events and memories in the life of my people. The water's murmur is the voice of my father's father. The rivers are our brothers. They quench our thirst. They carry our canoes and feed our children. So you must give the rivers the kindness that you would give any brother.

5   If we sell you our land, remember that the air is precious to us, that the air shares its spirit with all the life that it supports. The wind that gave our grandfather his first breath also received his last sigh. The wind also gives our children the spirit of life. So if we sell our land, you must keep it apart and sacred, as a place where man can go to taste the wind that is sweetened by the meadow flowers.

6   Will you teach your children what we have taught our children? That the earth is our mother? What befalls the earth befalls all the sons of the earth.

7   This we know: The earth does not belong to man, man belongs to the earth. All things are connected like the blood that unites us all. Man did not weave the web of life, he is merely a strand in it. Whatever he does to the web, he does to himself.

8   One thing we know: Our god is also your god. The earth is precious to him and to harm the earth is to heap contempt on its creator.

9   Your destiny is a mystery to us. What will happen when the buffalo are all slaughtered? The wild horses tamed? What will happen when the secret corners of the forest are heavy with the scent of many men and the view of the ripe hills is blotted with talking wires? Where will the thicket be? Gone!

10   Where will the eagle be? Gone!

When the last red man has vanished with this wilderness and his memory is only the shadow of a cloud moving across the prairie, will these shores and forests still be here? Will there be any of the spirit of my people left?

11   We love this earth as a newborn loves its mother's heartbeat. So, if we sell you our land, love it as we have loved it. Care for it, as we have cared for it. Hold in your mind the memory of the land as it is when you receive it. Preserve the land for all children, and love it, as god loves us. As we are part of the land, you too are part of the land. This earth is precious to us. It is also precious to you. One thing we know—there is only one god. No man, be he Red man or White man, can be apart. We are all brothers after all.

EXERCISE 2   Questions About the Reading

Select the letter that best completes each question or statement.

1. This passage centers on land and

   A. its animals.

   B. its forests.

   C. its future.

   D. its mystery.

2. Choose the sentence that tells the main idea.

   A. Humans should cherish and preserve the earth.

   B. President Pierce should not have bought the Indian's land.

   C. The earth belongs to Native Americans.

   D. The destiny of humans is a mystery.

3. According to the letter, Chief Seattle is least concerned about

   A. rivers.

   B. money.

   C. memories.

   D. buffalo.

4. From this passage it is implied that

   A. the white man was trying to cheat the Indians.

   B. the Indians had many agricultural traditions.

   C. Chief Seattle is willing to sell the land.

   D. Chief Seattle intends to visit the president in Washington.

5. The author probably wrote this letter

   A. to document his agreement with the president's wish to own land.

   B. to ask for a peace treaty that would safeguard the earth.

   C. to encourage the white man to care for the land as the Indian would.

   D. to explain the Indian's bond to the earth.

6. As used in this sentence, "What *befalls* the earth *befalls* all the sons of the earth," the word *befalls* means

   A. turns.

   B. happens to.

   C. befriends.

   D. angers.

EXERCISE 3   Sentence Explication

1. Either use the sentence that follows, or select and copy a different sentence from the reading selection.

   This we know: The earth does not belong to man, man belongs to the earth.

   paragraph #7

   Or the sentence you choose:

   _____

   _____

   paragraph #____

2. Paraphrase the sentence by rewriting it in your own words.

   _____

   _____

   _____

   _____

3. React to the sentence. What comments and questions do you have about it?

   _____

   _____

   _____

   _____

4. Relate to the sentence. What personal experiences does it bring to mind?

_____

_____

_____

_____

_____

EXERCISE 4   Questions for Writing and Discussion

1. What are three specific details in the letter that show the relationship between Native Americans and the land?

2. What does the letter attributed to Chief Seattle show about the chief?

3. If Chief Seattle did not write the letter, who might have written it? Why?

Working from Sentences to Paragraph

Rearrange Sentences with New Beginnings

There's a long, long trail a-winding
Into the land of my dreams,
Where the nightingales are singing
And a white moon beams.

— Stoddard King (b. 1913)

EXERCISE 5 Appalachian Trail

Part A

Use the provided new sentence beginnings to change the emphasis of the following sentences that tell about a 2,000-mile thru-hike. As you rearrange the words, be sure to keep the meaning of the original sentence.

1. People who enjoy hiking and viewing the beauty of the wilderness will find the Appalachian Trail, or AT, is a perfect path.

    The Appalachian Trail _____

    _____

    _____

2. The AT is a hiking trail that follows the ridge line of eastern America's Appalachian mountain chain.

    A hiking trail _____

    _____

    _____

3. The term "thru-hiking" means hiking the entire trail in one continuous journey.

    The meaning _____

    _____

    _____

4. Thousands of people attempt a thru-hike, but only one in ten people complete it.

    Although _____

    _____

    _____

5. On the summit of Springer Mountain in Georgia, the 2,160-mile trail begins, and on the summit of Mount Katahdin in central Maine, it ends.

   The 2,160-mile trail begins _____

   _____

   _____

6. The trail passes through fourteen states, eight national forests, and six national parks as it winds its way through the mountains.

   Winding _____

   _____

   _____

7. The entire trail is clearly marked with white blazes, two-inch-wide by six-inch-high rectangles painted on trees and rocks.

   Clearly marking _____

   _____

   _____

8. There is a series of three-sided lean-tos or shelters provided every 10 to 12 miles.

   Every 10 to 12 miles _____

   _____

   _____

9. Because 99 percent of the route is on publicly owned land, there is no fee charged, and no special permission is required to hike anywhere on the trail.

   Neither a fee nor _____

   _____

   _____

10. Parts of the AT are used by more than four million people annually.

More than _____

_____

_____

Part B

After checking your rearranged sentences with your instructor, copy them to create a paragraph.

Combine Sentences with New Beginnings

If future generations are to remember us with gratitude rather than contempt, we must leave them more than the miracles of technology. We must leave them a glimpse of the world as it was in the beginning, not just after we got through with it.

— President Lyndon B. Johnson
Upon signing the Wilderness Act of 1964

EXERCISE 6 Olympic National Park

Part A

Read the following draft of a paragraph describing a wilderness sanctuary that people can visit. In Parts B and C, you will work on combining sentences and adding transitions to make the paragraph coherent.

Olympic National Park is located in northwestern Washington. The park provides a place for solitude. The park provides a place for endless exploration. Olympic National Park is called "three parks in one." Tourists can see a glacier-capped mountain. Tourists can see a rain forest. Tourists can see an unspoiled coast. There are 266 glaciers. These glaciers crown the Olympic peaks. The park contains an undisturbed old-growth temperate[1] rain forest. This is the largest remaining rain forest in the Northwest. Precipitation in Olympic's rain forest ranges from 140 to 167 inches annually. The temperature seldom drops below freezing or rarely exceeds 80 degrees Fahrenheit. Olympic National Park has 60 miles of Pacific Ocean coastline. The coastline is the most primitive in the contiguous[2] United States. Many parts of Olympic National Park are accessible only by hiking trail. More than 95 percent of Olympic National Park is designated wilderness. The Wilderness Act of 1964 defined wilderness. It is a tract of undeveloped federal land of primeval character. It is where people are visitors who do not remain.

Part B

Combine the ideas from the sentences in each group to write one new sentence. Begin the new sentence using the indicated words. As you write the sentence, think about the emphasis and relationships you want to achieve.

1.

Olympic National Park is located in northwestern Washington.

The park provides a place for solitude.

The park provides a place for endless exploration.

Located in _____

_____

_____

2.

Olympic National Park is called "three parks in one."

Tourists can see a glacier-capped mountain.

Tourists can see an unspoiled rain forest.

Tourists can see a wild coast.

In Olympic National Park _____

_____

_____

---

[1] **temperate**   neither hot nor cold in climate
[2] **contiguous**   adjacent, bordering on each other

3.

There are 266 glaciers.

The glaciers crown Olympic peaks.

Crowning the Olympic peaks _____

_____

_____

4.

The park contains an undisturbed old-growth temperate rain forest.

This is the largest remaining rain forest in the Northwest.

The park _____

_____

_____

5.

Precipitation in Olympic's temperate rain forest ranges from 140 to 167 inches annually.

The temperature seldom drops below freezing or rarely exceeds 80 degrees Fahrenheit.

Annually, _____

_____

_____

6.

Olympic National Park has sixty miles of Pacific Ocean coastline.

The coastline is the most primitive in the contiguous United States.

Located on 60 miles _____

_____

_____

7.

Many parts of Olympic National Park are accessible only by hiking trail.

More than 95 percent of Olympic National Park is designated wilderness.

Because _____

_____

_____

8.

The Wilderness Act of 1964 defined wilderness.

It is a tract of undeveloped federal land of primeval character.

It is where people are visitors who do not remain.

As defined by the Wilderness Act _____

_____

_____

Part C

After checking your combined sentences with your instructor, copy them to create a paragraph. Add transitions to make the paragraph coherent. Note the differences between the original and the rewritten paragraphs.

Combine Sentences on Your Own

. . . the great Mississippi, the majestic, the magnificent Mississippi, rolling its mile-wide tide along, shining in the sun.

— Mark Twain (1835–1910)

EXERCISE 7   Mississippi River

Part A

Read the following draft of a paragraph describing the "Mighty Mississippi." In Parts B and C, you will work on combining sentences and adding transitions to make the paragraph coherent.

The Father of Waters begins as a humble trickle. It begins in the icy depths of Lake Itasca, Minnesota. The river continues on its journey south through the central United States. The journey ends some 2,000 miles away. This happens in the warm waters of the Gulf of Mexico. "Old Man River" is like a giant tree. It stretches its branches north, south, east, and west for nearly 3,000 miles. This happened in the early days on the new frontier. Thousands of flat-bottomed steamboats traveled up and down the Mississippi River. These steamboats were called paddle wheelers. The paddle wheelers carried passengers, cattle, produce, and cotton. The paddle wheelers received an enthusiastic welcome at ports along the Mississippi. Eventually, steamboat paddle wheelers became glamorous overnight excursion boats. They became fancy, highly ornate "wedding cakes on the water." These floating palaces had dining rooms. The dining rooms were magnificent. The dining rooms were decorated with exotic wood and velvet. Today, new steamboats continue river travel. Passengers listen to old river stories and jazz bands.

Part B

Revise the paragraph by combining the ideas from the sentences in each group to write one new sentence. As you write each sentence, think about the emphasis and relationships you want to achieve, adding transitions as needed.

1.

The Father of Waters begins as a humble trickle.

It begins in the icy depths of Lake Itasca, Minnesota.

_____

_____

_____

_____

2.

The river continues on its journey south through the central United States.

The journey ends some 2,000 miles away.

This happens in the warm waters of the Gulf of Mexico.

_____

_____

_____

_____

3.

"Old Man River" is like a giant tree.

It stretches its branches north, south, east, and west for nearly 3,000 miles.

_____

_____

_____

_____

4.

This happened in the early days on the new frontier.

Thousands of flat-bottomed steamboats traveled up and down the Mississippi River.

The steamboats were called paddle wheelers.

_____

_____

_____

_____

5.

The paddle wheelers carried passengers, cattle, produce, and cotton.

The paddle wheelers received an enthusiastic welcome at ports along the Mississippi.

_____

_____

_____

_____

6.

Eventually, steamboat paddle wheelers became glamorous overnight excursion boats.

They became fancy, highly ornate "wedding cakes on the water."

_____

_____

_____

_____

7.

These floating palaces had dining rooms.

The dining rooms were magnificent.

The dining rooms were decorated with exotic wood and velvet.

_____

_____

_____

_____

8.

Today, new steamboats continue river travel.

Passengers listen to old river stories and jazz bands.

_____

_____

_____

_____

Part C

After you have checked your sentences with your instructor, copy them to create a coherent paragraph. Note the differences between the original and the rewritten paragraphs.

Identify Sentences in Context

All sunshine makes a desert.

— Arabic proverb

EXERCISE 8   Death Valley National Park

The following paragraph about one of the hottest places on earth is missing periods. Add a period to mark the end of a sentence and capitalize the beginning word of the next sentence. Copy on the adjacent numbered line each word you have capitalized.

Located in southwestern California, Death Valley National Park covers almost 3,000 square miles the floor of the valley is almost 300 feet below sea level the valley floor is the lowest point in the Western Hemisphere and one of the hottest places on earth when the "forty-niners" entered the valley in 1849,

1. _____

2. _____

3. _____

4. _____

5. _____

6. _____

they were looking for a shortcut to the gold fields of
California in addition, other prospectors settled in the
valley mining for deposits of silver and other precious metals during the 1880s the "white gold of the
desert," borax, was discovered in a mine in Death
Valley borax was a popular all-purpose household
ingredient it kept milk sweet, softened water, aided
digestion, and helped clean clothes to get the borax
out of the mines, 20-mule-team borax trains hauled
loads weighing up to 46,000 pounds on a treacherous
journey of 165 miles to the railroad in Mojave neither
the presence of silver nor borax mines motivated set-
tlers to stay long enough to support a permanent community those who survived left the valley with the
words, "Good-bye, Death Valley," thus giving the
area its name.

7. _____
8. _____
9. _____
10. _____
11. _____
12. _____
13. _____
14. _____
15. _____
16. _____
17. _____
18. _____
19. _____
20. _____
21. _____
22. _____

Rearrange and Combine Sentences Using Transitions

*The Everglades is a test. If we pass it, we get
to keep the planet.*

— Joe Podger

EXERCISE 9   Everglades National Park

Part A

**Read a draft of an informative paragraph about a national park in danger of
extinction. In Parts B and C, you will work on combining, rearranging, and
adding transitions to make the paragraph coherent.**

The Everglades National Park is the largest remaining subtropical wilderness
in the United States. The Everglades is actually a river system. It is known as the

River of Grass. An unusual plant called sawgrass grows in its shallow water. The water in the Everglades is only a few inches deep. The Everglades River spreads almost 50 miles wide and 100 miles long, ending in the Gulf of Mexico. The Everglades National Park was once home to millions of creatures. It was a home for American alligators. It was a home for huge flocks of wading birds. At one time the birds numbered up to two and one-half million. Today, the Everglades is no longer a free-flowing river. Only one-tenth of the original wetland exists. The Everglades is an ecosystem threatened with extinction. Water flow is disrupted. Pollutants contaminate the wetland. Nonnative species invade the wetland. Some native species have virtually disappeared.

Part B

Revise the paragraph by using rearrangement, combining, and transitions *wherever appropriate* **to create new setnences. Not every sentence needs to be rewritten.**

1. The Everglades National Park is the largest remaining subtropical wilderness in the United States.

2. The Everglades is actually a river system.

3. It is known as the River of Grass.

4. An unusual plant called sawgrass grows in its shallow water.

5. The water in the Everglades is only a few inches deep.

6. The Everglades River spreads almost 50 miles wide and 100 miles long, ending in the Gulf of Mexico.

7. The Everglades National Park was once home to millions of creatures.

8. It was a home for American alligators.

9. It was a home for huge flocks of wading birds.

10. At one time the birds numbered up to two and one-half million.

11. Today, the Everglades is no longer a free-flowing river.

12. Only one-tenth of the original wetland exists.

13. The Everglades is an ecosystem threatened with extinction.

14. Water flow is disrupted.

15. Pollutants contaminate the wetland.

16. Nonnative species invade the wetland.

17. Some native species have virtually disappeared.

Part C

After you have checked your sentences with your instructor, copy them to create a paragraph. Note the differences between the original and the rewritten paragraphs.

Writing from Experience

EXERCISE 10   Write a Paragraph

Write a paragraph of 8–12 sentences on one of the following topics:

1. The United States provides numerous environments for the lover of the outdoors. Whether you live in the country, suburbs, or city, there is likely to be a variety of places you can go for fresh air. Explain where you go to enjoy the outdoors.

    Questions to Consider

    Where do you go? In what season do you most like to be in this place?

    Do you go by yourself or with others?

    What are the sights, sounds, tastes, and/or smells you experience?

    What is it that you enjoy most about this natural setting?

2. Travel agents try to make places seem inviting to encourage people to take trips. Assume the role of a travel agent. Describe a place with which you are familiar so that someone would like to see it.

    Questions to Consider

    What is the place?

    Where is it located?

What about the place is worth seeing?

Who especially would enjoy this place?

3. Places change over time. Describe a place that you have observed either worsening or improving. You may want to discuss a yard, a park, a neighborhood, or the exterior of a building.

   Questions to Consider

   What is the place?

   Where is it located?

   What did the place look like at first?

   How has it changed?

   Why has it changed?

4. Many organizations seek help in maintaining or restoring property and the land. Have you ever volunteered to help? Write about your experience.

   Questions to Consider

   Where did you volunteer? When did you volunteer?

   Why did you volunteer?

   How did your volunteer experience influence or change your perceptions?

   Why would or wouldn't you volunteer again in this same position?

For question 5, you are on your own to create questions for development.

5. The people of America are responsible for taking care of their great outdoors and the abundant natural resources with which this country has been blessed. Various campaigns stress the importance of cleaning up, using energy with care, and recycling whenever possible. Write about yourself as a steward of America's riches. During the past week, what have you done to help and/or harm the environment?

   Questions for Development

   _____

   _____

_____

_____

_____

For question 6, you are your own to decide a focus and to create questions for development.

6. Write on a topic of your choice about the American outdoors.

   Focus

   _____

   Questions for Development

   _____

   _____

   _____

   _____

EXERCISE 11   Revise Your Paragraph

Part A

Reread the paragraph you wrote for Exercise 10.

1. Choose one sentence to rearrange.

   Original Sentence _____

   _____

   Rearranged Sentence _____

   _____

2. Choose two or more sentences that could be effectively combined.

    Original Sentences

    _____

    _____

    _____

    _____

    Combined Sentences

    _____

    _____

    _____

You may want to use these revised sentences in the final draft of your paragraph.

Part B
Check your paragraph before submitting your final draft.

A CLEAR TOPIC SENTENCE
❐   Does the topic sentence state the topic?

❐   Does the topic sentence state what you will tell about the topic?

CONVINCING SUPPORT
❐   Do your sentences say what you want them to mean?

❐   Have you included enough details to make your ideas clear?

EFFECTIVE ORGANIZATION
❐   Does the paragraph have a beginning, a middle, and an end?

❐   Does your concluding sentence provide a summary of your main idea?

❐   Do you use transitions to link your ideas?

SUCCESSFUL SENTENCES

❐   Is each sentence complete?

❐   Have you eliminated run-ons and fragments?

❐   Have you written each word you need?

❐   Have you used a spell checker, speller, or dictionary to be sure words are spelled correctly?

❐   Have you used the correct form of homonyms?

EFFECTIVE TITLE

❐   Does your title suggest what the paragraph is about and make someone interested in reading it?

Writing from Resources

EXERCISE 12   Share Information

To answer these questions, visit the library or use a search engine on the Internet such as Lycos, Yahoo, or AltaVista. As you write your answers, use sentence rearrangement and combining techniques.

Your instructor will explain how to complete this section regarding the number of questions to answer and whether to work independently, with a partner, or in a group.

Appalachian Trail

1.   Where is the route of the Appalachian Trail? Highlight it on a map of the eastern United States. What is the highest elevation along the trail?

2.   What is the history of the Appalachian Trail?

3.   What are some practical facts about length of time, starting time, and cost for someone interested in a thru-hike? What is appropriate gear for somebody who intends to backpack for four days? Include food and items for meal preparation, sleeping gear, clothing, footwear, and backpacks.

Olympic National Park

4. What are the differences between a temperate and a tropical rain forest?

5. What is a glacier? Provide an illustration.

6. What plants are endemic to Olympic National Park?

7. What animals are endemic to Olympic National Park?

Mississippi River

8. What is the effect of flooding along the Mississippi River? What is the meaning of the following terms: flood plain, alluvial river, delta, and levees?

9. What are the purpose and the value of the Mississippi River Commission?

10. What is the origin of Samuel Clemens's penname Mark Twain? What did he write about the Mississippi River?

11. How has the Mississippi River influenced American music?

12. What vacation trips are offered for tourists who want to travel on the Mississippi River?

Death Valley National Park

13. What do people see when they go to Death Valley National Park (DVNP)?

14. What flora are found in Death Valley?

15. What fauna are found in Death Valley?

16. How did miners use 20-mule teams to remove borax?

17. What are the DVNP guidelines for people interested in backcountry hikes?

18. What is the story of the lost forty-niners?

Everglades National Park

19. What is the difference between endangered species and threatened species? Give examples.

20. What are the flora in the Everglades?

21. What are the fauna in the Everglades?

22. Why is the Everglades called "a park in danger"?

23. What efforts have been made to restore the Everglades' ecosystem?

24. What are the guidelines for backcountry camping in the Everglades?

More About the American Outdoors

25. What is wilderness ethics? Include guidelines while on a trail, in camp, for campfires, and for sanitation.

26. Why is biodiversity important for the future?

27. What is the Volunteer in Parks Program sponsored by the National Park Service? Who volunteers? What types of activities are involved? What is the process to volunteer in the NPS?

28. Which of the parks maintained by the National Park Service would you like to visit? Describe the park and explain what features about the park interest you.

EXERCISE 13   Understand Idioms

What is the meaning of each of the following idioms related to the outdoors? To find the meaning, check a dictionary or a specialized idiom dictionary, or ask someone who understands the idiom to explain it to you.

act down to earth

place in the sun

fall into place

sell down the river

up hill and over dale

stick in the mud

paddle one's own canoe

go take a hike

have one's ear to the ground

can't see the forest for the trees

green thumb

make a mountain out of a molehill

primrose path

pour oil on troubled waters

salt of the earth

tip of the iceberg

CHAPTER 10

The Information Age

There is a need to rethink and broaden the notion of lifelong education. Not only must it adapt to changes in the nature of work, but it must also constitute a continuous process of forming whole human beings. It should enable people to develop awareness of themselves and their environment and encourage them to play their social role at work and in the community.

— Jacques Delors

Longer lives and an increasingly complex environment challenge people today to keep on learning throughout their adult years. This chapter reading tells what has been learned about the oldest of old people.

Connecting Reading with Writing

EXERCISE 1   Reflections on the Information Age

1. What do people need to know today that they wouldn't have needed to know ten years ago?

    _____

    _____

    _____

2. How has the process of education, especially postsecondary education, become more flexible over the last ten years?

    _____

    _____

    _____

The Age of the Centenarian

The Charles A. Dana Foundation

1   When Willard Scott of NBC-TV started announcing 100th birthdays in 1980, only a handful of people applied for the honor of having their birthday celebrated on national television. In the 1990s he got hundreds of letters a month. These letters were from members of the country's most exclusive club: individuals with authenticated life spans of more than 100 years. And that club will be taking in many more new members in the coming decades. The twenty-first century will be the age of the centenarian.

2   Researchers at Bonn University in Germany who are studying longevity were asked to list the important factors in reaching a healthy 100 years of

age. Lists aren't the way to think about longevity,[1] they said. Instead, they suggested thinking about interactive patterns involving personality, intelligence, and behavior. Included as components[2] of those are activity, mood, adjustment, and social contact.

3   Genes do not seem to have a major influence on longevity. In one study, two populations with "genetic" differences in longevity turned out to differ from each other in ways we all readily recognize: diet, levels of physical activity, and national and ethnic antistress rituals. But even more significantly, the researchers found regional longevity affected by "national and ethnic traditions—that is, respectful attitude toward the elderly and involvement in bringing up children and in the solution of familial and even regional problems."

4   "People aren't likely to live long just because their parents did," according to Leonard Poon, who heads the University of Georgia's Centenarian Study. "It seems the genetic contribution is important for some centenarians who come from a long line of long-lived people. But we have as many centenarians who do not come from long-lived families." After studying more than 150 centenarians who have volunteered for the study, Poon is in an excellent position to know that good genes can only do so much toward helping you reach 100.

5   His findings do not support the widespread popular belief that consuming—or avoiding—certain foods promotes longevity. Perhaps Poon did not discern[3] a dietary component to longevity because today's centenarians grew into maturity during periods when less was known about the benefits of a good diet and the negative health consequences of a bad one. The majority of people in that generation who ate the same diet never reached the age of 100. The take-home lesson is this: The body does the best it can with whatever we put into our mouths. But if we are wiser about the foods we eat, our body has an easier time of it, and, as a secondary benefit, our chances for enhanced longevity are increased.

6   In support of this lesson, centenarians in Poon's study, whatever their diet, typically eat a wide variety of vegetables and take in more vitamin A and carotenoids than a control group of sixty- and eighty-year-olds. Moreover, many of the centenarians are now reversing some of their past unwise dietary choices. Poon and the nutritionist involved in the study, Mary Ann Johnson, found out that about 50 percent of centenarians in their group try now to avoid fats in their diets.

[1] **longevity**   long life

[2] **components**   parts, factors

[3] **discern**   recognize, determine

7   An additional surprise concerned the personality of the typical centenarian. Forget about the lamb-like dispositions and beatific[4] smiles of the stereotypical oldster that you're likely to encounter on a television commercial. Compared with younger groups, the centenarians are determined overall to have their own way. "They tend to be independent: They tend to dominate—they want their own way," Poon says. "As a result of living 100 years or more, centenarians have a wide variety of experiences behind them and have outlived spouses, friends, even their own children. Experts on the art of survival, centenarians score high on optimism; they are rarely depressed."

8   While centenarians share many things in common, differences outweigh similarities. Poon found his subjects differ in social and economic levels, education, work experience, religious beliefs, and level of prosperity. This, of course, is worth celebrating: It means that nobody has an exclusive[5] chance to live until 100.

9   A different study—the New England Centenarian Study—has also discovered something surprising. According to Thomas T. Perls, principal investigator of this study, "The centenarians I have met have, with few exceptions, reported that their nineties were essentially problem-free. As nonagenarians, many were employed, sexually active, and enjoyed the outdoors and the arts." Perls has observed that, after age ninety-seven, a person's chance of dying tends to veer[6] from the expected trend and actually becomes reduced. This supports his theory that the "oldest old" tend to be healthier than is traditionally believed. For reasons that no one understands, "some people are particularly resistant to acquiring the disorders that disable and kill most people before age ninety. Because of this resistance, not only do they outlive others, they do so relatively free of infirmities."[7] The key question is, of course: How do they do that?

10   No single factor stands out. Rather, reaching 100 years of age depends on a combination of factors. These include a genetic makeup that predisposes[8] to long survival, a positive attitude toward life, good stress-coping skills, health-promoting behaviors that reduce the risk of getting sick, sufficient common sense to deal with everyday problems of living, and, finally, the good fortune to avoid infectious diseases and serious injuries.

---

[4] **beatific**   innocent, saintly, adorable

[5] **exclusive**   special, private

[6] **veer**   turn around, change direction

[7] **infirmities**   illnesses, frailties

[8] **predisposes**   influences, biases

11   Can we really learn anything from people who were born before the first airplane flew, before women had the vote, before income taxes, before vitamins were known about? Yes, we can learn deliberately what they knew intuitively: Centenarians possess an intuitive knowledge of the difference between aging and becoming old. The difference? Becoming old means:

- Losing interest in life
- Accepting the notion that it's too late to change
- Believing that life doesn't matter anymore
- Failing to set goals and commitments
- Losing a sense of surprise and giving in to boredom

None of us can stop aging, but we don't have to grow old.

EXERCISE 2   Questions About the Reading

Select the letter that best completes each question or statement.

1. The passage is mostly about

    A. living 100 years.

    B. genes as a factor in longevity.

    C. diet as a factor in longevity.

    D. aging versus growing old.

2. Choose the sentence that tells the main idea.

    A. While centenarians share many things in common, differences outweigh similarities.

    B. Reaching 100 years of age depends on a combination of factors.

    C. None of us can stop aging, but we don't have to grow old.

    D. Centenarians possess an intuitive knowledge of the difference between aging and becoming old.

3. Which of the following is *not* mentioned in this passage as a factor in living to be 100?

    A. good genes

    B. positive work experiences

    C. healthy diet

    D. effective stress-coping skills

4. This passage suggests that

   A. Willard Scott enjoyed announcing birthdays of 100-year-olds.

   B. centenarians tend to be depressed and dependent on caretakers.

   C. people whose relatives lived to be 100 are likely to be 100, too.

   D. an individual has some personal influence in living a long life.

5. What statement would Leonard Poon's findings support?

   A. Little is known about the diets of today's centenarians.

   B. Certain foods seem to affect longevity.

   C. It does not matter what foods we eat.

   D. Many centenarians benefit from eating junk food and fat.

6. As used in the sentence, "Centenarians possess an *intuitive* knowledge of the difference between aging and becoming old," the word *intuitive* means

   A. carefree.

   B. studied.

   C. researched.

   D. instinctive.

EXERCISE 3   Sentence Explication

1. Either use the sentence that follows, or select and copy a different sentence from the reading selection.

   Compared with younger groups, the centenarians are determined overall to have their own way.

   paragraph #7

   Or the sentence you choose:

   _____

   _____

   paragraph #___

2. Paraphrase the sentence by rewriting it in your own words.

_____

_____

_____

_____

3. React to the sentence. What comments and questions do you have about it?

_____

_____

_____

_____

4. Relate to the sentence. What personal experiences does it bring to mind?

_____

_____

_____

_____

_____

EXERCISE 4   Questions for Writing and Discussion

1. What evidence does the author provide that suggests more people are living to be 100 years old and older?

2. According to Dr. Poon, what effect does diet have on longevity?

3. Based on the reading, what advice would you give to someone who wants to be a centenarian?

Working from Sentences to Paragraph

Rearrange Sentences with New Beginnings

Education is the best provision for old age.
— Aristotle (384–322 B.C.)

EXERCISE 5 Lifelong Learning

Part A

Use the provided new sentence beginnings to change the emphasis of the following sentences that explain the importance of flexibility in the job market. As you rearrange the words, be sure to keep the meaning of the original sentence.

1. No longer is the typical career path graduating from high school or college, working for a major corporation, and retiring from that corporation 30 years later.

   Graduating from high school _____

   _____

   _____

2. Nationwide in the 1990s, 14 million jobs were eliminated, while 15.5 million new jobs were created.

   Although nationwide in the 1990s _____

   _____

   _____

3. A worker, involved in lifelong learning and skills upgrading, is needed in today's workplace.

   Today's workplace needs _____

   _____

   _____

4. The impact of new information and communications technologies on the workplace is profound.

   New information and communications technologies have _____

   _____

   _____

5. The speed and power of microprocessors double roughly every 18 months, and data is dispatched in pico seconds and gigabits.

   As _____

   _____

   _____

6. A challenge for workers in the Information Age is keeping pace with new knowledge.

   Workers _____

   _____

   _____

7. People in the work force may change jobs more than 10 times before they reach retirement age.

   Before reaching retirement age _____

   _____

   _____

8. Regardless of their level of education, 75 percent of workers will require retraining in the future.

   Seventy-five percent of workers _____

   _____

   _____

9. People need to think of learning as a continuous pursuit not as a fixed event in order to survive in a rapidly changing society.

   Surviving _____

   _____

   _____

Part B

After checking your rearranged sentences with your instructor, copy them to create a paragraph.

Combine Sentences with New Beginnings

> *Once a new technology rolls over you,*
> *if you're not part of the steamroller,*
> *you're part of the road.*
> — Stewart Brand

EXERCISE 6   Digital Disk Technology

Part A

Read the following draft of an informative paragraph about a technology that has revolutionized our capacity to store information. In Parts B and C, you

will work on combining sentences and adding transitions to make the paragraph coherent.

In the early 1980s, digital disk technology became available. It began with the invention of the compact digital disk. The compact digital disk is called a CD. CDs were created as a replacement. They replaced records. The records were made of vinyl. CDs offered many advantages compared with vinyl records. There were no pops. There were no clicks. There were no hisses. These were problems associated with using records. A few years later another use for digital disk technology was recognized. This happened with the growth of the personal computer. This was a consequence. The CD-ROM was created. It was created as an information storage device. The CD stores the contents of books. The CD stores the contents of encyclopedias. The CD stores the contents of dictionaries. The CD stores computer programs. Another technology is the digital video disk. The digital video disk is also called the DVD. The DVD is used for playing movies rather than music. The DVD has tremendous storage capacity. It can store 18 trillion bytes of information.

Part B

Combine the ideas from the sentences in each group to write one new sentence. Begin the new sentence using the indicated words. As you write the sentence, think about the emphasis and relationships you want to achieve.

1.

In the early 1980s, digital disk technology became available.

It began with the invention of the compact digital disk.

The compact digital disk is called a CD.

Digital disk technology _____

_____

_____

_____

2.

CDs were created as a replacement.

They replaced records.

The records were made of vinyl.

CDs were _____

_____

_____

_____

3.

CDs offered many advantages compared with vinyl records.

There were no pops.

There were no clicks.

There were no hisses.

Compared with vinyl records, _____

_____

_____

_____

4.

A few years later another use for digital disk technology was recognized.

This happened with the growth of the personal computer.

With the growth _____

_____

_____

_____

5.

This was a consequence.

The CD-ROM was created

It was created as an information storage device.

Consequently, _____

_____

_____

_____

6.

The CD stores the contents of books.

The CD stores the contents of encyclopedias.

The CD stores the contents of dictionaries.

The CD stores computer programs.

The CD stores _____

_____

_____

_____

7.

Another technology is the digital video disk.

The digital video disk is also called the DVD.

The DVD is used for playing movies rather than music.

Another technology _____

_____

_____

_____

8.

The DVD has tremendous storage capacity.

It can store 18 trillion bytes of information.

With _____

_____

_____

_____

Part C

After checking your combined sentences with your instructor, copy them to create a paragraph. Add transitions and linking words to make the paragraph coherent. Note the differences between the original and the rewritten paragraphs.

Combine Sentences on Your Own

If you were going to die soon and had only
one phone call you could make, who would
you call and what would you say?
And why are you waiting?

— Stephen Levine

EXERCISE 7   From Party Line to the Internet

Part A

Read the following draft of an informative paragraph about the evolution of an invention that has revolutionized the way people can communicate with

one another. In Parts B and C, you will work on combining sentences and adding transitions to make the paragraph coherent.

Telephony has come a long way. It was invented in 1876. In the beginning of telephony this happened. People had to share telephone lines called "party lines." These telephone lines went to a central telephone office. The central office was staffed by operators. These operators made telephone connections. These operators made the connections manually using cords. In the early 1900s, automated switches replaced the cords. The switches used dial pulses to control relays. Later, computers interpreted dialed digits and made connections. The connections used electronic switches. In the late 1960s and early 1970s, new telephone services were established. These services included conferencing, call forwarding, and call waiting. In the 1980s, wireless radio technology was introduced. This technology allowed cellular telephones for mobile operation. During the 1990s, digital technology was applied to cell phones. This provided privacy on the cell phone. The cell phone and hand-held palm computer have merged into one device. This device simplifies making phone calls. This device retrieves and sends e-mail via the Internet. The Internet continues to merge with telephone networks. This merger will bring video imaging on the telephone. This merger will allow people to connect their phone directly to the computer.

Part B

Revise the paragraph by combining the ideas from the sentences in each group to write one new sentence. As you write each sentence, think about the emphasis and relationships you want to achieve, adding transitions as needed.

1.

Telephony has come a long way.

It was invented in 1876.

_____

_____

_____

_____

2.

In the beginning of telephony this happened.

People had to share telephone lines called "party lines."

These telephone lines went to a central telephone office.

_____

_____

_____

_____

3.

The central office was staffed by operators.

These operators made telephone connections.

These operators made the connections manually using cords.

_____

_____

_____

_____

4.

In the early 1900s, automated switches replaced the cords.

The switches used dial pulses to control relays.

_____

_____

_____

_____

5.

Later, computers interpreted dialed digits and made connections.

The connections used electronic switches.

_____

_____

_____

_____

6.

In the late 1960s and early 1970s, new telephone services were established.

These services included conferencing, call forwarding, and call waiting.

_____

_____

_____

_____

7.

In the 1980s, wireless radio technology was introduced.

This technology allowed cellular telephones for mobile operation.

_____

_____

_____

_____

8.

During the 1990s, digital technology was applied to cell phones.

This provided privacy on the cell phone.

_____

_____

_____

_____

9.

The cell phone and hand-held palm computer have merged into one device.

This device retrieves and sends e-mail via the Internet.

This device simplifies making phone calls.

_____

_____

_____

_____

10.

The Internet continues to merge with telephone networks.

This merger will bring video imaging on the telephone.

This merger will allow people to connect their phone directly to the computer.

_____

_____

_____

_____

Part C

After you have checked your sentences with your instructor, copy them to create a coherent paragraph. Note the differences between the original and the rewritten paragraphs.

Identify Sentences in Context

*A computer terminal is not some clunky old
television with a typewriter in front of it.
It is an interface where the mind and body
can connect with the universe and
move bits of it about.*

— Douglas Noel Adams

EXERCISE 8   The ENIAC

The following paragraph about one of the first computers is missing periods. Add a period to mark the end of a sentence and capitalize the beginning word of the next sentence. Copy on the adjacent numbered line each word you have capitalized.

In a large, well-ventilated room with drab-colored walls and open rafters, the first general purpose electronic computer, the Electronic Numerical Integrator and Computer, or ENIAC, stood it extended 150 feet in width with 20 banks of flashing lights that displayed the results of its computations ENIAC could add 5,000 numbers or do fourteen 10-digit multiplications in a second since the computer did not have the ability to store a program in its own memory,

1. _____
2. _____
3. _____
4. _____
5. _____
6. _____
7. _____
8. _____
9. _____

ENIAC had to be manually wired to execute a partic-	10. _____
ular program the major problem of the ENIAC was	11. _____
components that periodically failed during long peri-	12. _____
ods of operation with 17,480 tubes operating at a rate	13. _____
of 100,000 pulses per second, there would be 18 bil-	14. _____
lion chances of a failure occurring each and every	15. _____
second the ENIAC, developed in top secrecy during	16. _____
World War II, was completed too late to function in	17. _____
its original purpose of calculating firing tables for	18. _____
artillery weapons instead, in 1945 the ENIAC was	19. _____
used to perform millions of calculations related to	20. _____
top-secret studies of thermonuclear chain reactions—	21. _____
the hydrogen bomb this work paved the way for the	22. _____
modern computing industry.	23. _____

Rearrange and Combine Sentences Using Transitions

The palest ink is better than the best memory.

— Chinese proverb

EXERCISE 9   The Printing Press

Part A

Read a draft of an informative paragraph about an invention that changed the way people learned new ideas. In Parts B and C, you will work on combining, rearranging, and adding transitions to make the paragraph coherent.

This happened in 1450. Johannes Gutenberg invented the printing press. This press used moveable metal type. There were hundreds of individual metal letters. Gutenberg combined letters one by one. He put the letters on a special frame. This way he made a whole page of words. He inked individual metal letters. He pressed the inked type against a piece of paper. He printed pages one sheet at a time. This is what he did to print a different page. He arranged the individual letters on the frame. He was able to print about 300 pages a day. Before the invention of the printing press, only wealthy people could afford books. After the invention of the printing press, more people could afford to buy books. Masses of people had access to new information. The invention of the printing press changed society forever.

Part B

Revise the paragraph by using rearrangement, combining, and transitions *wherever appropriate* **to create new sentences. Not every sentence needs to be rewritten.**

1. This happened in 1450.

2. Johannes Gutenberg invented the printing press.

3. This press used moveable metal type.

4. There were hundreds of individual metal letters.

5. Gutenberg combined letters one by one.

6. He put the letters on a special frame.

7. This way he made a whole page of words.

8. He inked individual metal letters.

9. He pressed the inked type against a piece of paper.

10. He printed pages one sheet at a time.

11. This is what he did to print a different page.

12. He rearranged the individual letters on the frame.

13. He was able to print about 300 pages a day.

14. Before the invention of the printing press, only wealthy people could afford books.

15. After the invention of the printing press, more people could afford to buy books.

16. Masses of people had access to new information.

17. The invention of the printing press changed society forever.

Part C

After you have checked your sentences with your instructor, copy them to create a paragraph. Note the differences between the original and the rewritten paragraphs.

Writing from Experience

EXERCISE 10   Write a Paragraph

Write a paragraph of 8–12 sentences on one of the following topics:

1. During the past several decades, millions of workers have lost their jobs. Sometimes the loss of a job creates long-term difficulties for employees and their families. At other times, the loss of a job, although a temporary setback, brings new opportunities. Have you or anyone you know lost a job? If so, explain what effect the loss of the job had or is having on the person involved.

    Questions to Consider

    Who lost a job?

    What was the job? How long had the person had the job?

    Was the person satisfied with the job?

    Why did the person lose the job?

    How did the person react to the loss?

    What has happened in the long run? Or, what do you expect will happen?

2. Dr. Howard Gardner, a professor of education, psychology, and neurology, has identified a variety of human intelligences. He says people have abilities

in areas such as music, math and logic, language, spatial relationships, athletics, manual skills, social skills, personal skills, and appreciation of nature. In addition, according to Gardner, there may be areas of intelligence yet to be identified. Explain one of your intelligences, abilities, skills, or talents.

Questions to Consider

What is your area of strength?

When did you recognize you had it?

How do you use your strength?

Why is this strength helpful to you now?

How will it be part of your future?

3. Increasingly, Americans are becoming computer literate. Explain your level of computer literacy.

Questions to Consider

By your definition, are you a beginner, an intermediate, or an advanced user of the computer?

At what are you proficient? What more do you need or want to learn?

How have you learned to use the computer?

How will you learn more in the future?

For you, what are the advantages/disadvantages of using a computer?

4. Learning often occurs in the classroom. However, information and skills are also learned in other settings. Explain how you learned something or how you taught someone else something outside of the traditional classroom.

Questions to Consider

Who was the learner? Who was the teacher?

What was learned?

What was the process of the learning?

What was the reaction of the teacher?

What was the reaction of the student?

For question 5, you are on your own to create questions for development.

5. Not every person lives to be 100 years old, but chances are you know people in your family, in your community, or at your place of work who are much older than you are. Who is one of the oldest people you know?

Questions for Development

_____

_____

_____

_____

For question 6, you are your own to decide a focus and to create questions for development.

6. Write on a topic of your choice about the Information Age.

Focus

_____

Questions for Development

_____

_____

_____

_____

EXERCISE 11   Revise Your Paragraph

Part A
Reread the paragraph you wrote for Exercise 10.

1. Choose one sentence to rearrange.

    Original Sentence _____

    _____

    Rearranged Sentence _____

    _____

2. Choose two or more sentences that could be effectively combined.

    Original Sentences

    _____

    _____

    _____

    _____

    Combined Sentences

    _____

    _____

    _____

You may want to use these revised sentences in the final draft of your paragraph.

Part B

Check your paragraph before submitting your final draft.

A CLEAR TOPIC SENTENCE

❐ Does the topic sentence state the topic?

❐ Does the topic sentence state what you will tell about the topic?

CONVINCING SUPPORT

❐ Do your sentences say what you want them to mean?

❐ Have you included enough details to make your ideas clear?

EFFECTIVE ORGANIZATION

❐ Does the paragraph have a beginning, a middle, and an end?

❐ Does your concluding sentence provide a summary of your main idea?

❐ Do you use transitions to link your ideas?

SUCCESSFUL SENTENCES

❐ Is each sentence complete?

❐ Have you eliminated run-ons and fragments?

❐ Have you written each word you need?

❐ Have you used a spell checker, speller, or dictionary to be sure words are spelled correctly?

❐ Have you used the correct form of homonyms?

EFFECTIVE TITLE

❐ Does your title suggest what the paragraph is about and make someone interested in reading it?

Writing from Resources

EXERCISE 12 Share Information

To answer these questions, visit the library or use a search engine on the Internet, such as Lycos, Yahoo, or AltaVista. As you write your answers, use sentence rearrangement and combining techniques.

Your instructor will explain how to complete this section regarding the number of questions to answer and whether to work independently, with a partner, or in a group.

Lifelong Learning

1. What kinds of new jobs will be available in the next ten years? Which jobs will be most in demand?

2. What is the origin and meaning of "global marketplace"?

3. What is an elder hostel? Select one and tell about it.

4. How is asynchronous learning different from traditional learning? What are the advantages and disadvantages of asynchronous learning?

Digital Disk Technology

5. In what ways is digital technology used in the entertainment industry?

6. What is one advance in digital disk technology, other than used in the entertainment industry?

From Party Line to the Internet

7. What are current features available in telephones?

8. What are the problems associated with using a phone in a car? What legislation has been passed to regulate the use of a car phone?

The ENIAC

9. What is a computer programmer? What are the educational requirements for this job?

10. What is an information specialist? What are the education requirements for this job?

11. What is an abacus? How does it work?

12. How did the ENIAC assist in advancing weather forecasting?

13. What are the origins of electronic games? What is the latest trend?

14. What is Internet safety? Give examples.

The Printing Press

15. What is the Gutenberg Bible? What are its outstanding features?

16. What were Benjamin Franklin's contributions to printing? Read Benjamin Franklin's "Epitaph on Himself" (composed in 1728). Why is it significant?

17. What contributions did William Bullock make to printing?

More About the Information Age

18. How does a person determine if a web site contains valid information?

19. How have libraries changed as a result of the Information Age?

EXERCISE 13   Understand Idioms

What is the meaning of each of the following idioms related to the Information Age? To find the meaning, check a dictionary or a specialized idiom dictionary, or ask someone who understands the idiom to explain it to you.

read the fine print

on the record

closed book

bells and whistles

Trojan horse

at a ripe old age

have one's work cut out for one

Language Supplement

The Language Supplement is intended to provide you with some additional background and practice in usage and mechanics. It serves as a reference for finding answers to questions about language as they arise in your work. The practice exercises can help you master the skills you need for effective college and professional writing.

PARTS OF SPEECH

In English, words are divided into eight categories based on the way they function in a sentence. These eight categories, called **parts of speech,** are nouns, pronouns, verbs, adjectives, adverbs, prepositions, conjunctions, and interjections. Some word are used as several parts of speech. The word *box,* for instance, can be used as different parts of speech, depending on the sentence.

As a noun: He had a **box** to mail at the post office.

As a verb: The car was **boxed** in between the trucks.

As an adjective: She had a job at the **box** factory.

Nouns

Definition

A **noun** is a word used as the name of a person, place, thing, or idea.

Kinds

A **proper noun** is the name of a particular person, place, or thing.

John, Hannah, Long Island, Constitution

A **common noun** is the name of a person, place, thing, action, quality, or condition.

man, school, walk, greatness, happiness

A **concrete noun** is the name of a person, a place, or a thing that exists in space.

> school, child, tree

An **abstract noun** is the name of an idea, an action, a quality, or a condition that does not occupy space.

> goodness, growth, imagery

A **collective noun** is the name of a group of persons or things considered as one unit.

> class, crowd, mob

Properties

Gender indicates masculine, feminine, or neuter.

The masculine gender indicates the male sex.

> father, nephew, actor, stallion

The feminine gender indicates the female sex.

> mother, niece, actress, mare

The neuter gender indicates objects without gender.

> box, tree, car

Number indicates whether a noun names one thing or more than one thing.

Singular names one.

Plural names more than one.

The majority of nouns can be changed from singular to plural by adding *-s* or *-es*.

> key, keys; watch, watches; paper, papers

Some nouns have irregular plural forms.

> ox, oxen: foot, feet; tooth, teeth; deer, deer

A few nouns cannot be made plural because what they name cannot easily be counted.

> peace, faith, gratitude

Possessive case primarily shows ownership.

> Carolyn's music; Karin's job; doctor's patient

Pronouns

Definition

A **pronoun** is a word used in place of a noun.

Types of Pronouns	Examples
Personal	I, you, he, she, it, we, they, me, him, her, us, them, my, mine, your, yours, his, her, hers, its, our, ours, their, theirs
Relative	who, whose, whom, which, what, that
Indefinite	all, another, any, anyone, anybody, both, each, either, everyone, few, someone, many, neither, nobody, none, somebody
Interrogative	who? whose? whom? which? what?
Demonstrative	this, that, these, those
Reflexive	myself, yourself, yourselves, himself, herself, itself, ourselves, themselves

Personal pronouns are used to indicate the person speaking, the person spoken to, or the person spoken of.

> **I** have found that if **you** love life, life will love **you** back.
>
> — Arthur Rubinstein (1887–1982)

A **relative pronoun** refers to a preceding noun or pronoun, called an *antecedent*.

> The young man **who** has not wept is a savage, and the old man **who** will not laugh is a fool.
>
> — George Santanya (1863–1952)

(Young man is the antecedent of who; *old man* is the antecedent of who.)

Indefinite pronouns name an object or objects in general. Nouns, verbs, and other pronouns that refer to indefinite pronouns must agree with them in number. The indefinite pronouns that end in *body* or *one* are singular; *each, either, neither* are also singular.

The indefinite pronoun refers to an object or a person in a nonspecific manner.

From **each** according to his abilities, to **each** according to his needs.

— Karl Marx (1818–1883)

Interrogative pronouns are used to ask questions.

Who, or **why**, or **which**, or **what** is the Akond of Swat?

— Edward Lear (1812–1888)

Demonstrative pronouns point out which one or which ones.

This is the day which the Lord hath made; we will rejoice and be glad.

— Psalms 118:24

Reflexive pronouns help to clarify a preceding noun. When they are used for emphasis, they are called **intensive pronouns.**

Keep your promises to **yourself**.

— David Harold Fink

The **case** of a pronoun shows the pronoun's relationship to the rest of the sentence. The three cases of pronouns are the nominative, the objective, and the possessive.

Nominative Case	I, she, he, we, they, who, whoever
Objective Case	Me, him, her, us, them, whom, whomever
Possessive Case	My, mine, your, yours, his, her, hers, it, its, our, ours, their, theirs, whose

The case of a pronoun depends upon how it is used in a sentence. Notice how *we* becomes **us** in the objective case and **our** in the possessive case.

Nominative Case: **We** found the driver.

Objective Case: The driver found **us.**

Possessive Case: **Our** driver found the route.

Adjectives

Definition

An **adjective** is a word that describes a noun or pronoun.

> We must accept **finite** disappointment, but we must never lose **infinite** hope.
>
> — Martin Luther King, Jr. (1929–1968)

> You can't teach an **old** dog **new** tricks.
>
> — English proverb

Properties

One-syllable adjectives and some two-syllable adjectives add "–er" in comparing two things and "–est" in comparing three or more things. Some two-syllable adjectives and all longer adjectives are compared by adding *more* for two things and *most* for three or more. Negative comparisons are formed with the words *less* and *least*. Consult a dictionary when you are unsure which form to use.

> A **weak** mind is like a microscope, which magnifies trifling things but cannot receive great ones.
>
> — Philip Dormer Stanhope Chesterfield (1694–1773)

> He who has injured thee was **stronger** or **weaker** than thee. If **weaker**, spare him; if **stronger**, spare thyself.
>
> — Lucius Annaeus Seneca (4 BC–65 AD)

> A chain is as strong as its **weakest** link.
>
> — Danish proverb

Adverbs

Definition

Adverbs describe verbs, adjectives, or other adverbs. They often end in "–ly." Other common adverbs are *not, never, seldom,* and *often*.

> Be not afraid of growing **slowly**, be afraid of only standing still.
>
> — Chinese proverb

> Deceit **always** returns to its master.
>
> — French proverb

> In spite of everything, I **still** believe that people are **really** good at heart.
>
> — Anne Frank (1929–1945)

Properties

Adverbs, like adjectives, are compared using *more* and *most* and *less* and *least.*

> We **more frequently** fail to face the right problem than fail to solve the problem we face.
>
> — Anonymous

> We are **most nearly** ourselves when we achieve the seriousness of the child at play.
>
> — Heraclitus (c. 540 BC–c. 480 BC)

> Be modest! It is the kind of pride **least likely** to offend.
>
> — Jules Renard (1864–1910)

Prepositions

Definition

A **preposition** is a word used to show the relation of a noun or pronoun to some other word in the sentence. A preposition is followed by a noun or pronoun object to form a **prepositional phrase.**

Types

Direction	Position		Time	Other
along	above	beside	after	against
down	across	between	at	by
from	against	by	before	except
into	among	in	by	for
over	around	off	during	of
through	at	on	in	with
to	before	under	until	without
toward	behind	upon	within	
up	beneath	within		

Sentences may contain one prepositional phrase.

> **To a friend's house** the way is never long.
>
> — Danish proverb

Or, sentences may contain many prepositional phrases.

> **In the morning** be first up, and **in the evening** last to go **to bed**, for they that sleep catch no fish.
>
> — English proverb

Verbs

Definition

A **verb** is a word that expresses action or helps to make a statement. The main role of a verb is to show the tense or time of the sentence.

> A wise man **changes** his mind, a fool never **will**.
>
> — Spanish proverb
>
> We **are** what we believe we **are**.
>
> — Benjamin Cardozo (1870–1938)

Kinds

A **verb phrase** is made up of a main verb and one or more helping verbs.

> would have written
>
> am reading
>
> will have been married

Tense

The time expressed by a verb is its **tense.**
The **present tense** shows an action or state of being occurring now, at the present time. Present tense also shows habitual or ongoing action.

> No man **is** wise enough by himself.
>
> — Plautus (c. 254 BC–184 BC)
>
> The morning **has** gold in its mouth.
>
> — German proverb

Present perfect tense shows an action begun in the past and either just completed or still going on.

> If I **have seen** further, it is by standing on the shoulders of giants.
>
> — Sir Isaac Newton (1642–1727)
>
> Like all great travellers, I **have seen** more than I remember, and remember more than I **have seen**.
>
> — Benjamin Disraeli (1804–1881)

The **past tense** expresses action or state of being in the past that did not continue into the present.

> Necessity never **made** a good bargain.
>
> — Benjamin Franklin (1706–1790)

Past perfect tense shows an action finished in the past before another past action was begun.

> Piglet told himself that never in all his life . . . **had** he **seen** so much rain.
>
> — A. A. Milne (1882–1956)

Future tense shows an action that has not yet taken place.

> I **will begin** at the beginning.
>
> — Plato (c. 428 BC–c. 349 BC)
>
> This, too, **shall pass.**
>
> — William Shakespeare (1564–1616)

Voice

The verb is in the **active voice** when the doer of an action is the subject of the sentence.

> Haste **makes** waste.
>
> — English proverb

The verb is in the **passive voice** when the subject is the receiver of the action.

> Waste **is made** by haste.

Verbals

The **infinitive**, the main form of a verb, shows no tense. It consists of the word *to* followed by a verb. (If *to* is not followed by a verb, *to* is a preposition.)

> To everything there is a season, and a time to every purpose under the heaven. A time **to be born**, and a time **to die**, a time **to plant**, and time **to pluck** up what is planted. . . .
>
> — Ecclesiastes 3:1–8

The **gerund** is a verb acting as a noun. It ends in *ing*.

> **Caring** about others, **running** the risk of feeling, and **leaving** an impact on people, brings happiness.
>
> — Harold Kushner
> *When Bad Things Happen to Good People*, 1981

> **Seeing** is **believing**.
>
> — English proverb

The **participle** is a verb form that modifies a noun or pronoun like an adjective.

> . . . the fall of **dripping** water hollows the stone.
>
> — Lucretius (c. 98 BC–c. 55 BC)

> A **watched** pot never boils.
>
> — English proverb

> The **contented** person can never be ruined.
>
> — Chinese proverb

Conjunctions

Definition

A **conjunction** is a word that joins two words or two parts of a sentence.

Kinds

Coordinating conjunctions connect words, phrases, or clauses of equal rank. They are *and, but, for, nor, or, so,* and *yet.*

> One may have good eyes **and** see nothing.
>
> — Italian proverb

> Cold tea **and** cold rice are bearable, **but** cold looks **and** cold words are not.
>
> — Japanese proverb

Subordinating conjunctions connect clauses of unequal rank. They introduce dependent clauses. Some common subordinate conjunctions include *although, because, if, since, when,* and *until.*

> **If** you believe everything you read, you had better not read.
>
> — Japanese proverb

> **When** you blame others, you give up your power to change.
>
> — Douglas Noel Adams (b. 1952)

Correlative conjunctions connect words, phrases, or clauses of the same rank. They are used in pairs. The principal ones are *both . . . and, either . . . or, neither . . . nor, not only . . . but also, as . . . so.*

> The real problem is **not whether** machines think **but whether** men do.
>
> — B. F. Skinner (1904–1990)

> **Both** tears **and** sweat are salty, but they render different results. Tears will get you sympathy; sweat will get you change.
>
> — Jesse Jackson (b. 1941)

> **As** a man thinketh, **so** is he.
>
> — Proverbs 23:7

> Extreme fear can **neither** fight **nor** fly.
>
> — William Shakespeare (1564–1616)

Interjections

Definition

An **interjection** expresses strong feeling.

> **Ah**, but a man's reach should exceed his grasp—or what's a heaven for?
>
> — Robert Browning (1812–1889)

THE SENTENCE

Definition

A sentence contains both a subject and verb. It expresses a complete thought.

The Subject of a Sentence

The **subject** of a sentence names the person, place, thing, or idea that the sentence is about. The subject of a sentence is either a **noun** or **pronoun.** The subject of a sentence is not in a prepositional phrase.

The subject of the sentence is a *noun*.

> On a cold Lincoln's Birthday morning in 1908, six **automobiles** lined up in front of a cheering crowd in Times Square, New York City.

The subject of the sentence is a *pronoun*.

> **They** were about to start the longest and most difficult road race ever to be held—from New York to Paris.

Here or *there* is not the subject of a sentence.

> There was a small **group** of men who had great confidence in the cars they manufactured, owned, or drove.

A sentence may have a compound subject. In other words, several nouns or pronouns may serve as the subject.

> **Three French cars and one Italian car, one German car, and one car from the United States** participated in the race.

EXERCISE 1   Subjects

Underline the subject in each of the following sentences.

1. Crossing the ice of the frozen Bering Strait, they next raced across the vast expanses of Siberia and Russia.

2. After speeding through Europe, they finished their amazing seventeen-thousand-mile race in Paris.

3. Such a race was thought impossible for other reasons as well.

4. Roads were scarce and poorly made in those days.

5. Not many gas stations or garages were in existence.

6. The event started in the dead of winter, crossing the difficult open country and jagged mountains of three continents.

7. Ice, snow, swamps, and mud slowed and stopped the cars.

8. Also, few people lived along much of the lengthy route.

9. Widely separated telegraph stations were the only means of fast communication in most places.

10. There was a great deal of enthusiasm after the race.

The Verb of a Sentence

The **verb** is the word or group of words that tells the time of the sentence. The verb in a sentence works with the subject.

The form of the verb changes to show a change in time.

A verb may tell that the information in the sentence is in the past. Verbs ending in "–ed" are past tense verbs.

> Six automobiles **lined** up in front of a cheering crowd in Times Square, New York City.

A verb may indicate the information is at the present time.

> Six automobiles **line** up in front of a cheering crowd in Times Square, New York City.

> Six automobiles **are lining** up in front of a cheering crowd in Times Square.

A verb may show that the information is in the future.

> Six automobiles **will line** up in front of a cheering crowd in Times Square, New York City.

Verbs may show action or being or may link the subject with what comes after the verb.

A verb can show action.

> Six automobiles **lined** up in front of a cheering crowd in Times Square, New York City.

A verb can express a state of being.

The words *am, are, is, was, were, be, been,* and *being* are verbs.

> Roads **were** scarce and poorly made in those days.

A verb can link a subject with other words.

> The small group of men **seemed** confident in their cars.

Several words may be used as a verb phrase.

> The route of their rugged contest **had been planned** to take them across the United States to the West Coast, then north into Canada and Alaska.

> Courageous motorists **were preparing** to race their frail cars nearly around the world.

A verb may be compound; that is, several different verbs may work with one subject.

> The men **manufactured**, **owned**, or **drove** cars.

There may be more than one subject/verb combination in a sentence.

> But there **was** a small group of men who **had** great confidence in the cars they **manufactured, owned, or drove**.

EXERCISE 2 Subject and Verb

Draw one line under each subject and two lines under each verb.

1. The event started in the dead of winter.

2. Ice, snow, swamps, and mud slowed and stopped the cars.

3. No one before had tried to race across the United States.

4. The route of their rugged contest had been planned to take them across the United States to the West Coast, then north into Canada and Alaska.

5. From Alaska they would take a boat to Siberia.

6. This remarkable race took place during the very early days of the automobile.

7. Just sixteen years earlier, two Duryea brothers built the first successful gasoline automobile in the United States.

8. In 1908 a small group of men believed the automobile had an important future.

9. A few courageous motorists raced their frail cars nearly around the world.

10. Brass bands blared their national anthems to crowds of 250,000 New Yorkers.

Clauses

Definition

A **clause** is a group of words containing a subject and a predicate (verb).

A dependent clause does not make sense by itself.

When I took the test

An independent clause makes sense by itself and can stand alone.

I took the test.

Phrases

Definition

A **phrase** is a group of related words expressing a single idea. Since a phrase does not contain a subject and verb, it does **not** express a complete thought.

> in the trees
>
> with a little help
>
> to listen in silence
>
> finding time

EXERCISE 3   Sentence/Clause/Phrase

Identify each group of words by writing "sentence," "clause," or "phrase" on the given line.

_____ 1. could be called weather sensitive

_____ 2. I am positively in tune with the climate

_____ 3. if it's clear or overcast

_____ 4. while still lying in bed with my eyes closed

_____ 5. I feel out of sorts

_____ 6. when the barometer falls

_____ 7. during a hurricane last summer

_____ 8. as if the planet itself had come to a standstill

_____ 9. in an arid, mountainous part of the Northwest, a world of hot summers and cold, clear winters

_____ 10. about as perfect as a climate can get

_____ 11. after I moved north into the Willamette Valley of western Oregon

_____ 12. which has dank winters and somewhat unpredictable summers

_____ 13. there is often no rain at all in July

_____ 14. two years ago it rained or was overcast 22 out of 25 days

_____ 15. the clouds broke, the birds began to sing, and my bedroom filled with light

Types of Sentences

Definition

1. A **simple sentence** expresses a complete thought with a subject and verb.

Single subject and single verb

A clear conscience is a good pillow.
— French proverb

Single subject and compound verb

One may have good eyes and see nothing.
— Italian proverb

Compound subject and single verb

Man, woman, and love created fire.
— Spanish proverb

2. A **compound sentence** contains at least two clauses of equal rank. The two clauses are connected with a **coordinating conjunction** or a **semicolon**.

It is well that war is so terrible, **or** we should grow too fond of it.
— Robert E. Lee (1807–1870)

3. A **complex sentence** contains an independent clause and one or more dependent clauses. The two clauses are joined with a **subordinating conjunction**.

In the evening, **when** she was worn out with work, she had to lie on the hearth among the cinders.
— Grimms' Fairy Tales, *Cinderella*
Jacob Ludwig Karl Grimm (1785–1863)
Wilhelm Karl Grimm (1786–1859)

If we are to teach real peace in this world, and **if** we are to carry on a real war against war, we shall have to begin with the children.
— Mohandas Karamchand Gandhi (1869–1948)

Classification

1. A **declarative sentence** is one that states a fact or something assumed to be a fact.

    The strongest man on earth is he who stands most alone.
    — Henrik Ibsen (1828–1906)

2. An **interrogative sentence** is one that asks a question.

    When shall we meet again in thunder, lightning, or in rain?
    — William Shakespeare (1564–1616), *Macbeth*

3. An **imperative sentence** is one that expresses a command or an entreaty.

    Rapunzel, Rapunzel, let down your hair!
    — Grimms' Fairy Tales, *Cinderella*
    Jacob Ludwig Karl Grimm (1785–1863)
    Wilhelm Karl Grimm (1786–1859)

4. An **exclamatory sentence** is one that expresses surprise or deep emotion.

    Alas, how love can trifle with itself!
    — William Shakespeare (1564–1616)

Parallel Structure

Definition

Express parallel ideas in the same grammatical forms (nouns, adjectives, adverbs, verbs).

Parallel Nouns

Benevolence, righteousness, propriety, and **knowledge** are not infused into us from without.
— Mencius (c. 371 BC–289 BC)

Parallel Verbs

With that I **hurried** down the stairs with all the noise I could, **slipped** off my shoes, **ran** quietly along the gallery, **climbed** the front ladder, and **popped** my head out on deck.
— Robert Louis Stevenson (1850–1894)

The whole ship was **creaking, groaning, and jumping**.
— Robert Louis Stevenson (1850–1894)

Parallel Adjectives

> A great nose indicates a great man—**genial, courteous, intellectual, virile, courageous.**
>
> — Edmond Rostand (1868–1918), *Cyrano de Bergerac*

Parallel Clauses

> There are three arts which are concerned with all things: one which uses, another which makes, a third which imitates them.
>
> — Plato (c. 428 BC–c. 347 BC)

Parallel Phrases

> **By nature,** men are nearly alike; **by practice,** they get to be wide apart.
>
> — Confucius (c. 557 BC–479 BC)

EXERCISE 4   Parallel Structure

If a sentence has parallel parts, underline each of the parts. If a sentence lacks parallelism, mark an X on the line at the beginning of the sentence.

_____ 1. Many people like to hang posters in their bedrooms, living rooms, and on their office walls.

_____ 2. Favorite themes for posters include nature, celebrities, and automobiles.

_____ 3. Posters have been used since the fifteenth century to advertise products, publication of events, and to announce other information.

_____ 4. About 1800 the modern era of poster production began when industrialization created a need for extensive advertising and when the invention of lithography made it easier for artists to include colored illustrations on posters.

_____ 5. Later in the 1800s, a French artist, Jules Chéret, revolutionized the look of posters by making illustrations the dominant feature and reduced text to a limited role.

_____ 6. Chéret's methods introduced posters that were attractive, creative, and understandable even to illiterate people.

_____ 7. During World War I (1914–1918), governments used posters as propaganda instruments, to encourage army enlistment, and to sell war bonds.

_____ 8. Movie, travel, and beautiful posters became popular during the 1920s and 1930s.

_____ 9. Today entire shops are devoted to the sale of posters, prints, and frames.

_____ 10. To learn about posters, a person can study modern art in a college classroom, on the Internet, or through distance learning.

EXERCISE 5   Parallel Structure

If a sentence has parallel parts, underline each of the parts. If a sentence lacks parallelism, mark an X on the line at the beginning of the sentence.

_____ 1. The Museum of Modern Art (MoMA), located at 11 West 53 Street in New York City, is easily accessible on foot, by subway, and riding on the bus.

_____ 2. In this museum, the visitor can experience an impressive collection of modern and contemporary art.

_____ 3. In fact, from an initial gift of eight prints and giving of one drawing, the Museum of Modern Art's collection has grown to include more than 100,000 paintings, sculptures, drawings, prints, photographs, architectural models and drawings, and design objects.

_____ 4. Represented in the collections are paintings by Joan Miro, Claude Monet, Pablo Picasso, and canvasses painted by Jackson Pollock.

_____ 5. The collection also includes video, film, and other forms of art from 1880 to the present.

_____ 6. MoMA owns about 14,000 films and four million film stills and possessing as well 140,000 books, artist books, and periodicals.

_____ 7. People go to the museum to see paintings, to hear music, and taking courses.

_____ 8. Looking at the paintings and sculptures and sharing interpretations, both children and adults learn about art.

_____ 9. Museum staff are available for helping visitors locate materials or to answer their questions.

_____ 10. The Museum of Modern Art seeks volunteers familiar with twentieth-century art and who can speak at least two languages.

Modifiers

Definition

Modifiers are words that tell more about another word or words in a sentence. For clarity of meaning, place phrase and clause modifiers as close as possible to the words they modify.

> **Incorrect**   The damaged Thomas was crated and shipped back to the United States *coated with mud and grime from around the world.*

> **Correct**   The damaged Thomas, *coated with mud and grime from around the world*, was crated and shipped back to the United States.

> **Incorrect**   Spectators cheered loudly to encourage the motorists *watching the start.*

> **Correct**   *Watching the start,* spectators cheered loudly to encourage the motorists.

EXERCISE 6   Modifiers

For each correct sentence, write "correct" on the line before the sentence. If a sentence is incorrect, draw an arrow from the modifier to the word modified.

_____   1.   Mardi Gras is a pre-Lenten festival celebrated in Roman Catholic countries and communities known as Fat Tuesday.

_____   2.   Mardi Gras originated as one of carnival days held between Twelfth Night and Ash Wednesday in Roman Catholic countries with their origin in pre-Christian spring fertility rites.

_____   3.   Cities that have well-known modern Mardi Gras festivities are New Orleans, Louisiana; Rio de Janeiro, Brazil; Nice, France; and Cologne, Germany.

_____   4.   The festival includes Dixieland jazz, still played on Basin and Bourbon streets where Black musicians made it famous in the early 1900s in New Orleans.

_____   5.   The festivities, a period of fasting and penitence, are the last opportunity for merrymaking and indulgence in food and drink until after Lent.

_____   6.   Celebrated for a full week before Lent, extravagant parades, pageants, masked balls, and dancing in the streets take place during Mardi Gras.

_____ 7. Wearing a lace gown trimmed in ermine, the elegantly carpeted stairs were climbed by the costumed woman on her way to the masked ball.

_____ 8. Laughing confidently, the mask concealed her identity thought the woman.

_____ 9. Waving banners and throwing beads, the parade was enjoyed by the cheering children.

_____ 10. When staying in New Orleans, a traveler should not miss the Creole cooking.

EXERCISE 7 Modifiers

For each correct sentence, write "correct" on the line before the sentence. If a sentence is incorrect, draw an arrow from the modifier to the word modified.

_____ 1. In 1980, as they rebuilt the Congress Avenue Bridge in downtown Austin, Texas, bridge engineers beneath the bridge had no idea that the new crevices would make an ideal place for bats to roost.

_____ 2. As bats began moving in under the bridge by the thousands with fear, city residents reacted.

_____ 3. Members of Bat Conservation International began to teach people that bats are gentle and incredibly sophisticated animals.

_____ 4. Bats, including mosquitoes, eat from 10,000 to 30,000 pounds of insects each night.

_____ 5. The people of Austin in honor of their bats began to appreciate the largest urban bat colony in North America and even erected a sculpture.

_____ 6. Making nightly flights, residents and tourists alike appreciate the more than 1.5 million bats.

_____ 7. The bats arrive in mid-March and return to Mexico in early November.

_____ 8. They emerge at different times every night, but the hotter and drier the weather gets, the earlier they set out for food.

_____ 9. August is the best viewing month because the newborn bats come out with their mothers, and the newborn bats are just beginning to fly.

_____ 10. The pink, hairless babies with a wingspan of up to a foot grow to be about three to four inches long.

Agreement of Subject and Verb

Definition

A verb is either singular or plural to match its subject.

When a singular word is used as a subject, the verb is singular. Notice that singular verbs end in "s."

> A tart tongue never **mellows** with age, and a sharp tongue **is** the only edge tool that **grows** keener from constant use.
>
> — Washington Irving (1783–1859), *Rip Van Winkle*

When a plural word is used as a subject, the verb is plural.

> Evils **draw** men together.
>
> — Aristotle (384 BC–322 BC)
>
> These **are** the times that try men's souls.
>
> — Thomas Paine (1737–1809), *Common Sense* 1776

Locate the subject before choosing whether to make a verb singular or plural.

The subject of a sentence is not in a prepositional phrase.

> From the errors of others, a wise **man** corrects his own.
>
> — Pubililius Syrus (?–42 BC)

The subject may come after the verb.

> Under every stone lurks a **politician.**
>
> — Aristophanes (c. 448 BC–385 BC)

Note: The words *there* and *here* are **never** the subject of a sentence.

> There are some **remedies** worse than the disease.
>
> — Pubililius Syrus (?–42 BC)

EXERCISE 8   Subject/Verb Agreement

Read each of the following sentences for subject/verb agreement. If a sentence is correct as written, write "correct" on the line. If a sentence has an error, underline the subject and write the correct form of the verb on the line.

_____ 1. Numismatics is a hobby that involves collecting coins and paper money.

_____ 2. There is some people who collect only American coins.

_____ 3. An old American coin, which was made at one of the official mints in the United States, are often valuable.

_____ 4. United States coins has a date and a mint mark to show when and where they was made.

_____ 5. An important component in assessing the value of coins are the coin's condition.

_____ 6. There is some numismatists having coins with nearly every date, mint mark, and variation in design.

_____ 7. Collectors reads coin newsletters, attends auctions and conventions, and joins clubs to discuss coin values.

_____ 8. The largest organization of coin collectors in the world are the American Numismatic Association, founded in 1891.

_____ 9. The U.S. Mint has physical custody of the U.S. government reserves of precious metals.

_____ 10. The U.S. Mint produce special coins, including American Eagle gold coins, and national medals.

EXERCISE 9   Subject/Verb Agreement

Read each of the following sentences for subject/verb agreement. If a sentence is correct as written, write "correct" on the line. If a sentence has an error, underline the subject and write the correct form of the verb on the line.

_____ 1. A study of genealogy, which is the study of a family's ancestors, often results in the creation of a family tree.

_____ 2. People, regardless of their age, researches their family history for many reasons.

_____ 3. Many researchers want to know "Who am I?" and "Where did I come from?"

———— 4. A person with children like to establish the roots of family history and bring history to life.

———— 5. Actually, genealogical studies, if taken seriously, create a sense of personal pride and understanding.

———— 6. Family units that have been fragmented and separated is reconnected.

———— 7. A family history provides a legacy for future generations to build on.

———— 8. Both amateur and professional researchers is able to gain knowledge, have fun, and meet other people with similar interests.

———— 9. For treating some diseases, genealogical information are helpful.

———— 10. Some genealogists, doing background research for a filmmaker or author, makes fascinating finds.

Agreement of Pronoun and Antecedent

Definition

An **antecedent** is a word or word group to which a pronoun refers. A pronoun agrees in number with its antecedent.

Locate the antecedent before deciding whether to use a singular or plural pronoun.

When an antecedent is singular, the pronoun is singular.

> An example from the **monkey**: the higher **it** climbs, the more you see of **its** behind.
> — Saint Bonaventure (c. 1217–1274)
> We cannot command **nature** except by obeying **her**.
> — Sir Francis Bacon (1561–1626)

When an antecedent is plural, the pronoun is plural.

> **Dictators** ride to and fro upon tigers that **they** dare not dismount.
> — Sir Winston Spencer Churchill (1874–1965)

Use a singular pronoun to refer to indefinite pronouns, such as *anyone, anybody, everybody, either.*

> **Everyone** blames **his** memory, but never **his** judgment.
> — French proverb

Use a plural pronoun when two or more antecedents are joined by *and.*

> **Power and authority** are sometimes bought by kindness, but **they** can never be begged as alms by an impoverished and defeated violence.
>
> — Edmund Burke (1729–1797)

Use a singular pronoun when two or more antecedents are joined by *nor.*

> Neither a wise man **nor** a brave man lies down on the tracks of history to wait for the train of the future to run over **him**.
>
> — Dwight David Eisenhower (1890–1969)

Use either a singular or a plural pronoun with a collective noun depending on whether the collective noun is used in a singular or a plural sense.

Collective noun used in the singular sense

> All happy families resemble one another, but each unhappy **family** is unhappy in **its** own way.
>
> — Leo Tolstoy (1817–1875)

Collective nouns used in the plural sense

> You don't choose your **family**. **They** are God's gift to you, as you are to **them**.
>
> — Desmond Tutu (b. 1931)

EXERCISE 10   Pronoun Agreement

Indicate the correct pronoun for each sentence. Be ready to explain your choice of pronoun.

1. Ballooning can be an exhilarating experience for adventurers if (he, she, they) want a magic carpet ride.

2. From the inexperienced beginner to the seasoned veteran, a ride in the clouds has (its, their) thrills.

3. The balloons with (its, their) beauty, exhilaration, and tranquility have enthusiasts from the young to the not-so-young.

4. Before a balloon takes off, motorized fans do (its, their) work of inflating it.

5. When a balloon is filled with air, propane burners heat (it, them).

6. The launching process takes about thirty minutes, and then the balloon is ready for (its, their) flight.

7. Once the balloon is inflated, the traveler will join (his/her, their) pilot in a beautiful oversized, handcrafted wicker basket.

8. Even though the balloon is moving five or six miles per hour, travelers can almost not feel (it, them) moving.

9. Pilots generally fly close to the ground, usually under 400 feet, so (he/she, they) can point out the sights.

10. Balloonists are advised to have (his/her, your, their) cameras ready to take excellent photographs from an unobstructed 360-degree view.

EXERCISE 11   Pronoun Agreement

If a sentence is correct, write "C" on the line before the sentence. Where there are errors in pronoun agreement, draw a line through an incorrect pronoun and write the correct form of the pronoun on the line.

1. Over three thousand years ago, Chinese craftsmen made kites using bamboo for their frame and silk for the sail and bridle.

2. A kite is known for their mythical and religious dimensions and also its scientific importance.

3. American diplomat and scientist Benjamin Franklin experimented with kites in his investigation of atmospheric electricity.

4. The American physicist and inventor Alexander Graham Bell also used kites in their studies.

5. Box kites, consisting of its two or more connected open-ended boxes, were used for sending meteorological instruments.

6. In 1903, Samuel Franklin Cody actually crossed the English Channel itself on a vessel towed by kites.

_____ 7. In the late nineteenth and early twentieth centuries, kites were used for lifting military observers to heights from which he/she could observe the disposition of enemy forces.

_____ 8. Today, two main groups fly kites for its sport and entertainment.

_____ 9. Stunt kites, lightweight and versatile, are used by its owners to perform tricks of which there are no limit.

_____ 10. Because they are able to withstand strong winds, power kites are used for kite flying and kite sailing, both dangerous sports that appeal to their enthusiasts.

PUNCTUATION

Purpose of Punctuation

Punctuation helps express clear written thought. The importance of punctuation can be illustrated by the following sentences. Notice how changing the punctuation changes the meaning.

An English professor wrote the words, "a woman without her man is nothing," on the blackboard and directed the students to punctuate them correctly.

The men wrote "A woman without her man is nothing."

The women wrote "A woman: without her, man is nothing."

Punctuation Rule	*Examples*
COMMA	
Use a comma to separate *words* in a series.	In thy face I see the map of honor, truth, and loyalty. — William Shakespeare (1564–1616)

Use a comma to separate *phrases* in a series.	He has plundered our seas, ravaged our coasts, burned our towns, and destroyed the lives of our people. — Thomas Jefferson (1743–1826)
Use a comma to separate *clauses* in a series.	I came, I saw, and I conquered. — Julius Caesar (100 BC–44 BC)
Use a comma to separate a *word* preceding the subject of a sentence from the rest of the sentence.	Peace, it is peace that must guide the destinies of peoples and of all mankind. — Pope Paul VI (1897–1978)
Use a comma to separate a *phrase* preceding the subject of a sentence from the rest of the sentence.	Being the third son of the family, my head began to be filled very early with rambling thoughts. — Daniel Defoe (1660–1731), *Robinson Crusoe* To me, party platforms are contracts with the people. — Harry S. Truman (1884–1953)
Use a comma to separate a *clause* preceding the subject of a sentence from the rest of the sentence.	When it is dark enough, you can see the stars. — Charles Austin Beard (1874–1948) If you don't scale the mountain, you can't view the plain. — Chinese proverb
Use a comma to set off a *noun in apposition,* a noun that renames what has come before.	Happiness, that grand mistress of ceremonies in the dance of life, impels us through all its mazes and meanderings but leads none of us by the same route. — Albert Camus (1913–1960)

Use a comma to separate a *short direct quotation* from the rest of the sentence.

"Many happy returns of the day," said Piglet.

— A. A. Milne (1882–1956)

Use a comma to separate *parenthetical expressions* from the rest of the sentence.

A great writer is, so to speak, a second government in his county.

— Aleksandr Isayevich Solzhenitsyn (b. 1918)

Money, it is said, is the root of all evil.

— Folk saying

The fault, dear Brutus, is not in our stars, but in ourselves.

— William Shakespeare (1564–1616), *Julius Caesar*

Use a comma to separate a *nonrestrictive clause* from the word it modifies. (A nonrestrictive clause is one that does not limit the meaning or add anything important to the idea of the sentence.)

My father, who was very ancient, had given me a competent share of learning, as far as house-education and a country free school generally goes.

— Daniel Defoe (c. 1660–1731), *The Life and Adventures of Robinson Crusoe* 1791

Use a comma to separate clauses joined by *and, but, for, so, yet,* and *or.*

Give a little love to a child, **and** you get a great deal back.

— John Ruskin (1819–1900)

A slip of the foot you may soon recover, **but** a slip of the tongue you may never get over.

— Benjamin Franklin *(1706–1790), Poor Richard's Almanac*

Hold tenderly that which you cherish, **for** it is precious, **and** a tight grip may crush it.

— Bob Alberti

Contemplate thy powers, contemplate thy wants and thy connections, **so** shalt thou discover the duties of life and be directed in all thy ways.

— Akhenaton
(c. 1350 BC–c. 1334 BC)

We worry about what a child will be tomorrow, **yet** we forget that he is someone today.

— Anonymous

Destroy the seed of evil, **or** it will grow up to your ruin.

— Aesop (c. 620 BC–c. 560 BC)

Use commas to separate the *parts of a date.*

They will be married on Saturday, January 15, 2006, in their hometown.

Use commas to separate the *parts of an address.*

Write to Janice at 810 Michigan Avenue, Chicago, Illinois.

SEMICOLON

Use a semicolon to separate the clauses of a compound sentence when there is no conjunction.

Life is very short and very uncertain; let us spend it as well as we can.

— Ben Johnson (b. 1961)

Use a semicolon to separate the parts of a compound sentence when these parts have commas within themselves.

Fear less, hope more; eat less, chew more; whine less, breathe more; talk less, say more; hate less, love more, and all good things will be yours.

— Swedish proverb

Use a semicolon between clauses of a compound sentence that are joined by *therefore, hence, however, nevertheless, moreover, accordingly, besides, also, thus, then, still,* and *otherwise.*

Man is always more than he can know of himself**; consequently,** his accomplishments, time and again, will come as a surprise to him.

— Golo Mann (b. 1909)

I imagine**; therefore,** I belong and am free.

— Emily Dickinson (1830–1886)

COLON

Use a colon to separate a long quotation or a list from the rest of the sentence.

All books are divisible into two classes**:** the books of the hour and the books of all time.

— John Ruskin (1819–1900)

PARENTHESES

Use parentheses to enclose a remark that might be omitted without altering the sense of the sentence.

He (William Gladstone) speaks to me as if I was a public meeting.

— Queen Victoria (1819–1901)

DASH

Use a dash as a substitute for parentheses to indicate something added to the sentence without being necessary to its meaning.

What gives life its value you can find—and lose.

— Dag Hammarskjold (1905–1961)

Circumstances—what are circumstances? I make circumstances.

— Napoleon Bonaparte (1822–1891)

APOSTROPHE

Use an apostrophe and an "s" to indicate the possessive case for nouns.

A man's character is his fate.
— Heraclitus
   (c. 540 BC–c. 475 BC)

Use an apostrophe to indicate the omission of a letter or letters.

Beggars can't be choosers.
— English proverb

Don't count your chickens before they hatch.
— English proverb

Use an apostrophe to form the plural of numbers and letters and words considered as nouns.

Mind your p's and q's.
— Early American saying

QUOTATION MARKS

Use quotation marks to enclose the exact words of a speaker or writer. Periods and commas are placed inside quotation marks.

"It isn't fair, it isn't right," Mrs. Hutchinson screamed, and then they were upon her.
— Shirley Jackson (1916–1965),
   The Lottery

Question marks and exclamation points are inside or outside of the quotation marks depending on whether they are part of the quoted material.

"Never, never!" whispered she. "What we did had a consecration of its own."
— Nathaniel Hawthorne
   (1804–1864), *The Scarlet Letter*

A quotation within a quotation is set off by single quotation marks.

"Breathes there a man with soul so dead
Who never to himself hath said,
'This is my own, my native land.'"

— Sir Walter Scott (1771–1832)

Use quotation marks to enclose a quoted title.	One of the most famous American short stories is Edgar Allen Poe's "The Tell-tale Heart."
Use quotation marks to indicate a word itself, not its meaning.	Define "friendship."
	You must dot your "i's" and cross your "t's."

EXERCISE 12   Commas

If a sentence is correct, write "C" on the line before the sentence. Where commas need to be added, write the commas where they are needed and circle the commas. If a comma is not needed, mark an X through the comma.

_____ 1. Before the federal government was established in Washington, D.C., George Washington lived in New York City, and at Mount Vernon, Virginia.

_____ 2. "The White House," said the brochure "was the first public building erected in Washington, D.C."

_____ 3. The White House, the official residence of the president of the United States was built between 1792 and 1800.

_____ 4. The address of the White House is 1600 Pennsylvania Avenue Washington, D.C.

_____ 5. The White House has also been known as the President's Palace the President's House and the Executive Mansion.

_____ 6. When Theodore Roosevelt had *The White House* engraved on his stationery in 1901 the name became official.

_____ 7. George Washington did not live in the White House but he gave the approval to have it built.

_____ 8. On the ground floor are cloakrooms, a china room, the kitchen, and the library.

_____ 9. The president's private apartments occupy the second floor of the main building and the third floor consists chiefly of guest rooms and quarters for the staff.

_____ 10. On the first floor are the formal rooms of state, which are open to the public.

EXERCISE 13   Commas

If a sentence is correct, write "C" on the line before the sentence. Write commas where they are needed and circle the commas. Mark an X through any comma that is unnecessary.

_____   1.   One of the stately rooms in the White House the East Room is used for state receptions and balls.

_____   2.   One of the guides said "The bodies of William McKinley and John F. Kennedy lay in state in the East Room."

_____   3.   Your guests Mr. President will join you for dinner in the Blue Room.

_____   4.   In the Red Room as most people are aware, the First Lady receives guests.

_____   5.   Additions to the original building including the low-lying terraces or pavilions, were constructed in 1807 during the administrations of Thomas Jefferson.

_____   6.   Importantly Lyndon B. Johnson in 1964 issued an executive order establishing the Committee for the Preservation of the White House.

_____   7.   Putting her own look on the second-floor apartments, Mrs. Lady Bird Johnson decorated her bedroom in greens and yellows and she set up a comfortable working space from which she directed her many activities.

_____   8.   When the Carters lived in the White House young Amy Carter the daughter of Jimmy and Rosalynn had a tree house in the gnarled old cedar on the south lawn.

_____   9.   From the earliest times to the present each presidential family has put the stamp of its personality on the White House a national treasure belonging to the people of America.

_____   10. Visitors are encouraged to take a 15-to-20 minute walk-through tour of the White House scheduled most Tuesdays through Saturdays from 10 A.M. until noon.

EXERCISE 14   Semicolons

If a sentence is correct, write "correct" on the line before the sentence. Write semicolons where they are needed, and circle the semicolons. Mark an X through misused semicolons.

_____   1.   The fifth largest of the earth's seven continents is Antarctica; it is located almost entirely south of the Antarctic Circle, surrounding the South Pole.

_____ 2. Antarctica is the coldest continent with the lowest temperature ever recorded anywhere on earth, −89.2° C (−128.6° F) the continent is also buffeted by winds as high as 200 mph.

_____ 3. Antarctica has no native population its only residents are scientists and research teams.

_____ 4. The land is more than 95 percent ice covered; and contains about 70 percent of the world's fresh water.

_____ 5. Marine life in the waters surrounding Antarctica is currently being studied this marine life includes whales and krill, a tiny, shrimp-like animal.

_____ 6. Economic development of Antarctica does not seem likely however, using resources from the continent may be possible in the future.

_____ 7. The interior of Antarctica has almost continuous daylight during the Southern Hemisphere's summer; likewise, there is almost continuous darkness during the Southern Hemisphere's winter.

_____ 8. Plants are restricted to small ice-free areas; animals live on land and in the water.

_____ 9. Scientists in 1985 discovered that a so-called ozone hole develops each Antarctic spring in the stratosphere high above the continent they also discovered that the hole more or less disappears by the end of the season.

_____ 10. Geologists have now seen most of the exposed rock areas of the continent they continue increasing their knowledge of the basic geologic structure and history of Antarctica.

EXERCISE 15   Semicolons

If a sentence is correct, write "correct" on the line before the sentence. Insert semicolons where they are needed, and circle the semicolons. Mark an X through misused semicolons.

_____ 1. On April 6, 1909, Robert Peary believed he was the first person to stand at the North Pole; at the northernmost spot of the world— 90 degrees North latitude.

_____ 2. Some skeptics say Peary never actually reached the North Pole; in fact, he may have been 50 miles from the Pole.

_____ 3. The Arctic region covers more than 14 million square kilometers it is slightly larger than one and a half times the size of the United States.

_____ 4. The Arctic Ocean is the world's fourth largest ocean; it is smaller only than the Pacific, Atlantic, and Indian Oceans.

_____ 5. The cold climate in the Arctic area has continuous dark days during the winters and continuous daylight in the summer.

_____ 6. The area has supplies of oil and gas in addition, fish and other marine mammals, such as seals and whales, inhabit the area.

_____ 7. The economy is based on exportation of the natural resources however ships have difficulty navigating the Arctic Ocean from October to June when the area is virtually ice locked.

_____ 8. There are no submarine cables for telephone service and only limited networks of air, water, and land routes throughout the region.

_____ 9. The Northwest Passage across North America and the Eurasian Northern Sea Route provide main travel routes during the summer important ports include Prudhoe Bay (United States), Churchill (Canada), and Murmansk (Russia).

_____ 10. The frozen Arctic region is a stark, barren land, a land of strange, silent beauty, and a compelling destination for adventurous travelers.

EXERCISE 16   The Apostrophe

Proofread the following sentences for apostrophes. If a sentence is correct, write "correct' on the line. When an apostrophe is needed, write the word and its apostrophe on the line before the sentence.

_____ 1. Johann Sebastian Bach, born on March 21, 1685, wasnt an ordinary musician.

_____ 2. He was one of his fathers excellent music students.

_____ 3. When Johann Bach became the organist in Weimar, he began practicing promptly each day by six oclock.

_____ 4. Taking a three months leave, Bach studied with a renowned Danish-born organist and composer, Dietrich Buxtehude.

_____ 5. Bachs first wife died in 1720, and the next year he married Anna Magdalena Wilcken, a fine singer and daughter of a court musician.

_____ 6. The thirteen children produced by this second marriage and the seven from his first marriage had opportunities to study music from the childrens exercise books written by Bach.

_____ 7. During his later years at St. Thomass Church in Leipzig, he squabbled continually with the town council, which didnt appreciate his musical genius and saw in him little more than a stuffy old man who clung stubbornly to obsolete forms of music.

_____ 8. Nonetheless, the 202 surviving cantatas that he wrote in Leipzig havent gone out of style and are still played today.

_____ 9. Bachs sight began to fail in the last years of his life, and he died on July 28, 1750, after undergoing an unsuccessful eye operation.

_____ 10. Its the expressiveness of Bachs music, particularly his vocal works, that touches listeners everywhere.

EXERCISE 17 The Apostrophe

Proofread the following sentences for apostrophes. If a sentence is correct, write "correct' on the line. When an apostrophe is needed, write the word with the apostrophe on the line before the sentence.

_____ 1. The Grateful Deads appeal extended worldwide to millions of people who enjoyed their work.

_____ 2. Many people, however, were taken aback by the medias portrayal that both the band and their followers were obsessed with drugs and the 1960s.

_____ 3. The sixties marked the bands starting point.

_____ 4. During the three decades they played together, the bands accomplished musicians impressed audiences and critics with the quality of their playing and composing.

_____ 5. For their fans, the Grateful Dead projected love and reverence without violence or cheap commercialism.

_____ 6. Thousands of the groups supporters, the Deadheads, as theyre called, traveled in old buses, vans, and cars to follow their band.

_____ 7. The Grateful Dead, insisting on musical quality, built the worlds largest high-fidelity sound reinforcement system.

_____ 8. In addition, the Grateful Dead developed a light show pushing technologys limits.

_____ 9. With more than 300 songs in their repertoire, the Grateful Dead played thousands of times all over the country as well as in Europe and Africa.

_____ 10. Its Jerry Garcia who was at the heart of the group that moved tens of thousands of people at each concert to respond enthusiastically to the rhythm of the music.

CAPITALIZATION

Capitalization is a form of emphasis.

RULES FOR CAPITALIZATION

Capitalize the first word of every sentence.	**We** hold these truths to be self-evident, that all men are created equal, that they are endowed by their Creator with certain unalienable Rights, that among these are Life, Liberty, and the pursuit of Happiness. — Declaration of Independence
Capitalize the names of days of the week, months of the year, and holidays. (Do not capitalize the seasons.)	**Tuesday**, **June**, **Thanksgiving**, fall, winter, summer, spring
Capitalize all proper nouns and adjectives.	**English**, **French**, **Italian**, **Spanish**, **Hebrew**, **Chinese**, **Christian**, **Jewish**, **Mohammedan**
Capitalize titles of honor and respect, when such titles are part of a name.	The audience rose to greet **General Mac Arthur**. Another general accompanied him.
Capitalize the names of points of the compass when they indicate a section of the country.	Henry Clay said, "I know no **North**, **South**, or **East**, or **West**." It is the great north wind that made the Vikings. — Scandanavian proverb
Capitalize the first word and all important words in a title.	Bertrand Russell wrote "**An Inquiry into Meaning and Truth**."

Capitalize the first word of a direct quotation.	Susan B. Anthony spoke of equal rights for women when she said, "**It** is downright mockery to talk to women of their enjoyment of the blessings of liberty while they are denied the ballot."
Capitalize abbreviations of titles, degrees, or honors written after an individual's name.	Albert Einstein, **Ph.D.**, devised the theory of relativity. Thanks to Jonas Salk, **M.D.**, we have the polio vaccine.
Capitalize the name of anything personified.	Because I could not stop for **Death He** kindly stopped for me. — Emily Dickinson (1830–1886)
Capitalize the first word of every line of poetry.	**The** music in my heart I bore **Long** after it was heard no more. — William Wordsworth (1770–1850)
Capitalize the pronoun "I" and the interjection "O."	**O**! for a Muse of fire that would ascend the brightest heaven of invention! — William Shakespeare (1564–1616)
Capitalize every name or title of the Deity and every pronoun referring to the Deity.	Life is **God**'s novel. Let **Him** write it. — Isaac Bashevis Singer (1904–1991)

EXERCISE 18 Capitalization

Capitalize words as necessary in the following sentences.

_____ 1. One day last february i read a book about dancers.

_____ 2. I learned that one of the most influential american choreographers, dancers, and teachers during the twentieth century was martha graham.

_____ 3. Martha Graham, born in pittsburgh, pennsylvania, received her early training under ruth st. denis and ted shawn at the denishawn school.

_____ 4. she directed the dance department at the eastman school of music in rochester, new york, and danced in broadway productions in new york city.

_____ 5. american composers aaron copland and william schuman composed music for her dances.

_____ 6. Having created more than 150 works, graham retired as a dancer in 1970.

_____ 7. When she was 90, she choreographed _rite of spring_ by russian-american composer igor stravinsky.

_____ 8. The instructor said, "you should read this book about dancers."

_____ 9. The student asked her instructor, dr. bentley, if she could write a paper about martha graham.

_____ 10. The paper is due on halloween, october 31.

EXERCISE 19 Capitalization

Capitalize words as necessary in the following sentences.

_____ 1. Arthur ashe was one of the most prominent tennis players in united states history.

_____ 2. He began playing tennis as a boy in richmond, virginia.

_____ 3. At ucla, where he had a tennis scholarship, arthur ashe gained national recognition.

_____ 4. In 1963, arthur ashe represented the united states in davis cup play, an important honor.

_____ 5. He won both ncaa individual and team championships in 1965 before he graduated in 1966 with a ba in business administration.

_____ 6. Ashe and several other players formed the atp (association of tennis professionals), an organization that worked to provide top players with large sums of prize money.

_____ 7. When ashe wanted to play in the south african open, the union of south africa denied his visa because of the color of his skin.

_____ 8. In 1975, at the age of 31, arthur ashe won the wimbledon tournament, becoming the number one tennis player in the world.

_____ 9. Following heart surgery, he retired in 1980 to become a commentator for hbo sports and abc sports, a columnist for *the washington post* and *tennis* magazine, and author of *a hard road to glory*, his autobiography.

_____ 10. After the public learned he was hiv-positive as a result of blood transfusions, arthur ashe spent the rest of his life educating people about aids before he died on february 6, 1993.

EXERCISE 20   Quotation Marks

Punctuate each of the following sentences as needed. Use quotation marks, commas, periods, and other punctuation.

_____ 1. You wouldn't believe the rodeo near Bozman said Becca.

_____ 2. Rob asked do you know that the word rodeo comes a Spanish word meaning roundup?

_____ 3. The five major rodeo events, added Becca, are saddle bronco riding, bareback bronco riding, bull riding, steer wrestling, and calf roping.

_____ 4. Wait a minute Dick interrupted what is a bronco?

_____ 5. Rob responded quickly a bronco is a frisky horse that wants to get rid of its rider.

_____ 6. Riders in a rodeo must be very skilled said Becca.

_____ 7. The excitement of the stands she continued keeps everyone at attention.

_____ 8. Rob asked Becca if she knew how rodeos got their start.

_____ 9. Becca said there have been rodeos since the mid-1800s when cattle were driven to be sold at markets in the larger towns and cowhands got together to show their skills.

_____ 10. Becca and Rob agreed it was a good tradition.

EXERCISE 21   Quotation Marks

Punctuate each of the following sentences as needed. Use quotation marks, commas, periods, and other punctuation.

_____ 1. Becca informed the class that although the dinosaur became extinct, a contemporary, the alligator has survived to the present.

_____ 2. In 1987, she continued, the American alligator became the official state reptile of Florida.

_____ 3. Rob stated that when Spanish explorers saw this creature in America, they named it *el lagarto*, the lizard.

_____ 4. I know, he said, alligators live even where the water is of poor quality, and they are common in rivers, lakes, marshes, ponds, ditches, and even salt water.

_____ 5. Becca said, when the animals are at least four feet long, they are generally safe from predators.

_____ 6. Although alligators prefer to eat carrion, she added, they eat almost anything, even sticks, stones, fishing lures, and aluminum cans.

_____ 7. Rob said alligators have been hunted for meat and skins ever since people arrived in Florida.

_____ 8. Today's laws allow alligators to be harvested during controlled hunts Becca said and alligators are raised in captivity for the production of meat and skins.

_____ 9. In fact she added a multimillion-dollar alligator industry generates approximately 300,000 pounds of meat and 15,000 skins each year.

_____ 10. Becca and Rob concluded that an alligator's awesome appearance and threatening jaws are signals that approaching an alligator closely is not safe.

HOMONYMS AND WORD PAIRS

Learn to distinguish between homonyms and word pairs that sound alike, or nearly alike, but have different meanings.

advice, advise

Advice means "information" or "guidance."
Advise means "to give information or advice."

> The instructors gave us good *advice.*
>
> Instructors *advise* their students to watch certain videos.

affect, effect

Affect means "to influence."
Effect means "result."

> Alcohol *affects* the brain negatively.
>
> The pharmacist expects the *effects* of the antibiotic to be beneficial.

all ready, already

All ready means "completely prepared."
Already means "before" or "previously."

> The accountants were *all ready* for the income tax season.
>
> These accountants had *already* passed their CPA exams.

brake, break

Brake means "stop."
Break means "come apart."

> To pass state inspection requirements, the motorcycle needed new *brakes.*
>
> If a tree limb falls on a windshield, the glass may *break.*

coarse, course

Coarse means "rough."
Course means "direction," "part of a meal," or "school subject."

> The chef's *coarse* language offended the wait staff.
>
> My *course* of action today is to prepare the soup *course* for my cooking *course.*

have, of

Have is often used in the phrase "might *have*."

Of shows relationship as in the "the pages *of* the book."

> If people had helped Burns, instead of talking about him, he might *have* become a greater poet. Several volumes *of* his poetry are in the library.

hear, here

Hear means "to sense with the ear."

Here means "in this place."

> Did you *hear* the new sound band?
> The band will play *here* in the auditorium this evening.

hole, whole

Hole means an "empty spot."

Whole means "complete or entire."

> The tiny dog fell into a *hole.*
> The *whole* neighborhood gathered to see the dog rescued.

its, it's

Its means "belonging to it."

It's means "it is."

> The dog injured *its* leg.
> When that program is over, the children know *it's* time for bed.

knew, new

Knew is the past tense of "know."

New means "not old."

> Bridgette *knew* she wanted to be a dental hygienist.
> The dental office was outfitted with *new* equipment.

know, no

Know means "to understand."

No is "not positive."

> A new employee must *know* company policies.
> One company policy is that an employee will make *no* personal calls during work hours.

loose, lose

Loose means "free, not fastened."

Lose means "to part with accidentally."

> The clasp on my purse was *loose.*
>
> How did you *lose* your wallet?

passed, past

Passed means "handed to," "succeeded in," or "went by."

Past means "at some time before now."

> Jeremy *passed* the bar exam on this second try.
>
> During the *past* week, the lawyer tried two cases in county court.

peace, piece

Peace means "serenity or calmness."

Piece means "a part of."

> *Peace* of mind is supreme happiness.
>
> The baker was pleased to have his guests try a *piece* of pumpkin pie.

plain, plane

Plain means "simple."

Plane means "aircraft" or "flat surface."

> The solution of getting transportation to the airport was *plain,* not complicated.
>
> The family would not take a *plane*; they would rent a minivan to drive to Grandma's birthday party.

principal, principle

Principal means "main" or "person in charge of a school."

Principle means "law" or "standard."

> The physical education teacher is taking courses so that she can become a *principal.*
>
> Stretching before exercising is an important *principle.*

quiet, quite

Quiet means "silent."

Quite means "completely."

> When the movie began, the theater became *quiet.*
>
> The movie was *quite* violent.

right, write

Right means "correct" or "the opposite of left."

Write means to "put to pen and paper" or "compose using words."

> I believe that it is *right* to take a *right* turn on to Main Street.
>
> Please *write* the directions for me so that I will not get lost.

than, then

Than joins two parts of a comparison.

Then means "at that time."

> Try to find a chair that is smaller *than* this one.
>
> *Then* we will have a chair to fit in the corner.

their, they're, there

Their (belonging to them) shows ownership.

They're means "they are."

There means "in that place."

> My neighbors are celebrating *their* thirtieth wedding anniversary.
>
> *They're* planning a large party.
>
> I hope to be *there.*

threw, through

Threw is the past tense of "throw."

Through means "finished" or "from one side to the other."

> The governor *threw* the first pitch in the first baseball game of the season.
>
> The lieutenant governor, walking *through* the crowd of spectators, shook many hands.

to, too, two

To shows relationship between two things.

Too means "excessively" or "also."

Two is a number.

> The *two* of them went *to* the mall *too* late for the sale.

wear, where

Wear means "to have on."

Where means "in what place?"

> What do people *wear* on Friday dress-down days?
>
> *Where* are you going to find that kind of clothing?

weather, whether

Weather means "atmospheric conditions."

Whether means "if," "if it happens that," or "in case."

> The prediction is for cold, rainy *weather*.
>
> If the *weather* is inclement, the group will have to decide *whether* to attend the celebration.

whose, who's

Whose (belonging to whom) shows ownership.

Who's means "who is."

> *Whose* car is in the driveway?
>
> *Who's* there?

you're, your

You're means "you are."

Your means "belonging to you."

> Do not send the e-mail until *you're* certain that it is complete.
>
> What is *your* e-mail address?

EXERCISE 22   Homonyms

Choose the correct word and be able to tell why it is correct.

1. Felix and Marie wish to go to the city to see (their, there, they're) friends.

2. After traveling by motorcycle across the country, Claire had (advice, advise) for other travelers.

3. Jennifer is going to (right, write) an editorial for the morning newspaper.

4. Is that (your, you're) jacket on the floor?

5. Conesha walked (passed, past) her friends without stopping to talk.

6. Jason is taller (than, then) his brother Joshua.

7. Brett will (know, no) many of the people at the conference.

8. What will you (wear, where) to the formal dinner party?

9. At five o'clock, the mechanic was not (quiet, quite) finished tuning up the car.

10. (Who's, Whose) your professor?

11. During the violent storm, the boat broke (loose, lose) from its moorings.

12. My neighbor's children ran (threw, through) the bushes to greet me.

13. The owners had to take care of (there, their, they're) property.

14. We want to go to the movies (to, too, two).

15. The (plain, plane) truth is that the price has increased because manufacturing costs have risen.

16. The (affect, effect) of all my studying has been good grades and a fine education.

17. Kim's (principal, principle) reason for arriving early is to have some (quiet, quite) to get her work done.

18. By next year, Gerard may (have, of) finished his (coarse, course) work.

19. In January, tourists expect skiing (weather, whether).

20. Every morning Janice has a bowl of cereal and a (peace, piece) of toast.

EXERCISE 23   Homonyms

Proofread the following sentences checking for correct word forms. Write the correct form.

1. Chad wonders weather to where his raincoat to school today.

2. The workers threw the lose shingles into the vacant lot passed the garage.

3. The children are particularly quite when their in the cafeteria.

4. Is it true that Evelyn is going to right to Ann Landers for advise?

5. Your taller then anyone else in your family.

6. Our principle reason for traveling by plane is to get to Australia as soon as we can.

7. Chewing on the caramel, Tim may of lost a peace of his tooth.

8. As soon as he saw them, George new the puppies were already for a walk.

9. Can you here the brakes squeal when I turn a corner?

10. The coarse in basic computing has been useful during my hole college career.

SPELLING RULES

Learning some of the important rules in spelling can be helpful.

Terms

vowels: the letters *a, e, i, o, u,* and sometimes *y*

consonants: any letters that are not vowels

syllable: a part of a word pronounced as a unit, consisting of a vowel alone or with one or more consonants

one syllable words:	do, the, an
two syllable words:	mat/ter; hap/py
three syllable words:	con/sist/ing; syl/la/ble
four syllable words:	A/mer/i/can; Al/a/bam/a

accent: a special emphasis given to a syllable in a word.

Rule	Examples	Exception
I before *e* except after *c*	achieve, believe, bier, brief, hygiene, grief, thief, friend, grieve, chief, fiend, patience, pierce, priest, ceiling, conceive, deceive, perceive, receipt, receive, deceit, conceit	*E* before *i* The combined vowels are pronounced as long *a.* neighbor, freight, beige, sleigh, weight, vein, weigh
When adding an ending to a word that ends with a silent *e*, drop the final *e* if the ending begins with a vowel.	advance + ing = advanc-ing surprise + ing = surpris-ing store + age = storage desire + ous = desirous like + able = likable dense + ity = density	Keep the final *e* if there is a *c* or *g* before the silent *e.* notice + able = noticeable courage + ous = coura-geous

When adding an ending to a word that ends with y, change the y to i when it is preceded by a consonant.	supply ➤ supplies
	worry ➤ worried
	merry ➤ merrier
	body ➤ bodily
	rely ➤ reliance
	crafty ➤ craftiness
		Keep the final y if
		(a) the word ends in -ing.
		  cry ➤ crying
		  study ➤ studying
		(b) the final y is preceded
		  by a vowel.
		  obey ➤ obeyed
		  say ➤ saying

When adding an ending that begins with a vowel to a one-syllable word; double the final consonant if the last three letters of the word are consonant/vowel/ consonant.	sad ➤ sadder shop ➤ shopper quit ➤ quitter hum ➤ humming thin ➤ thinnest plan ➤ planned	Do not double the final consonant in a one-syllable word if the final letter of the word is h or x. high ➤ higher box ➤ boxer
When adding an ending that begins with a vowel to a multiple-syllable word; double the final consonant if the accent falls on the last syllable.	prefer ➤ preferred propel ➤ propelled admit ➤ admitted commit ➤ committee transfer ➤ transferring excel ➤ excelled control ➤ controlled begin ➤ beginning	

Add *s* to form the plural of a noun. Add *–es* to words ending in *ch, sh, ss, x,* or *z.*

toe ➤ toes
row ➤ rows
match ➤ matches
fish ➤ fishes
class ➤ classes
box ➤ boxes

(a) Nouns ending in *y,* drop the *y,* and add *-es.*
try ➤ tries
duty ➤ duties
(b) Nouns ending in *f* or *fe,* change the *f* or *fe* to *ve* and add *-s.*
knife ➤ knives
wolf ➤ wolves
life ➤ lives

Add prefixes
Adding a prefix to a word does not change its spelling.

mis + spell = misspell
dis + appoint = disap-
    point
dis + satisfy = dissatisfy
un + necessary = unneces-
    sary

Appendices

A: Sentence Rearrangement

	Sentence Openers	Common Pattern	Sentence Variety
1	Invert the order of the words in a sentence.	The race car drivers *were fearless.*	*Fearless were* the race car drivers.
		The Tin Lizzie was *the most dependable automobile of its day.*	*The most dependable automobile of its day* was the Tin Lizzie.
2	Move *a group of related words* to the beginning of the sentence.	Two jet engines pushed a 10-ton monster *across Nevada Black Rock Desert* at more than 766 miles per hour.	*Across Nevada Black Rock Desert,* two jet engines pushed a 10-ton monster at more than 766 miles per hour.
		Six automobiles lined up *on February 12, 1908,* to start the most difficult road race.	*On February 12, 1908,* six automobiles lined up to start the most difficult road race.
3	Start the sentence with a word that answers the question *how*.	The detective *thoroughly* inspected the skid marks left by the car.	*Thoroughly,* the detective inspected the skid marks left by the car.
		The team *carefully* greased the frozen metal before touching it.	*Carefully,* the team greased the frozen metal before touching it.
4	Start the sentence with a word that answers the question *when*?	Indiana was *soon* covered with the deepest snow of the race.	*Soon* Indiana was covered with the deepest snow of the race.
		The food froze *quickly* in temperatures of twenty-seven degrees below zero.	*Quickly,* the food froze in temperatures of twenty-seven degrees below zero.

5	Start the sentence with a word that answers the question *where*.	Thousands of people lined the streets *everywhere* to cheer the racers on.	*Everywhere*, thousands of people lined the streets to cheer the racers on.
		The Canadians raced *here* on Monday.	*Here*, the Canadians raced on Monday.
6	Start the sentence with a word that answers the question *how much* or *to what extent*.	The snow came down *endlessly*.	*Endlessly*, the snow came down.
		In 1908 drivers *often* had vehicle mishaps.	*Often*, drivers had vehicle mishaps in 1908.
7	Start the sentence with *to* and the verb next to it.	The race must be completed in an hour *to avoid the approaching storm*.	*To avoid the approaching storm*, the race must be completed in an hour.
		It is important *to send* the message.	*To send* the message is important.
8	Start the sentence by changing a verb to end in *-ing*.	John *turned* to his right and saw the flashing lights.	*Turning* to his right, John saw the flashing lights.
		The writer *speaks* with authority and convinces her audience to action.	*Speaking* with authority, the writer convinces her audience to action.
9	Start the sentence by using *one of the verbs* in the sentence.	George Schuster was *determined* to win the race, and he drove through the night.	*Determined* to win the race, George Schuster drove through the night.
		The Americans were *overwhelmed* by the blowing, stinging sand, so they cut eye-holes in their handkerchiefs to wear as face shields.	*Overwhelmed* by the blowing, stinging sand, the Americans cut eye-holes in their handkerchiefs to wear as face shields.

| 10 | Change the order of a group of related words beginning with words such as *although, because, since, after, when, if.* | The road continued to twist and double back on itself *even after the cars drove through the rice fields.* | *After the cars drove through the rice fields,* the road continued to twist and double back on itself. |
| | | The bridge sagged and swayed *although the racers removed as much weight as possible from the car.* | *Although the racers removed as much weight as possible from the car,* the bridge sagged and swayed. |

B: Sentence Combining

	Technique	*Examples*	*Combined*
1	Join two sentences using *and, but, or, for, so, yet.*	The De Dion crossed first. The Zust followed.	The De Dion crossed first, *and* the Zust followed.
		Scarfoglio decided to drive up the hills. The mechanic backed the car up to get a good start.	Scarfoglio decided to drive up the hills, *so* the mechanic backed the car up to get a good start.
2	*Join closely related* ideas.	We found the door. We could not open it.	We found the door *but* could not open it.
		They continued to race. They continued on Monday.	They continued to race on Monday.

3	Combine single words from sentences without any changes in word form.	The changes in the routes caused confusion. The confusion was *great*.	The changes in the routes caused *great* confusion.
		The racers drove up the hill. The racers were *exhausted*. The hill was *steep*.	The *exhausted* racers drove up the *steep* hill.
		Linden soaked his feet in the stream. His feet were *aching*. His feet were *swollen*. The stream was *cold*. The stream was *clear*.	Linden soaked his *aching, swollen* feet *in* the *cold, clear* stream.
4	Combine single words from sentences with changes in word forms.	Don't drive that car. It leaks.	Don't drive that *leaky* car.
		John was able to fix our radiator. It had a *leak*.	John was able to fix our *leaking* radiator.
		Carol stared at the fender. It had a *dent*.	Carol stared at the *dented* fender.
		The rain started at noon. It was *sudden*.	The rain *suddenly* started at noon.
5	Combine groups of words from sentences without changes in form.	The raceway is being torn down. The raceway is *near the hospital*.	The raceway *near the hospital* is being torn down.

		A puff of smoke appeared. It appeared *above the hood.* The smoke was inky *black.*	A puff of inky *black* smoke appeared *above the hood.*
6	Add a group of words to a sentence separating the group with a comma or pair of commas.	Chaffer headed the race crew of the De Dion. Chaffer was *Commissioner-General of the race.*	Chaffer, *Commissioner-General of the race,* headed the race crew of the De Dion.
		The third French entry was the smallest car in the race. It was a *one-cylindar car.*	The third French entry, a *one-cylinder car,* was the smallest car in the race.
7	Add a group of words to a sentence by changing the form of the first word.	Here are the results. We *took* the results from the newspaper.	Here are the results *taken* from the newspaper.
	The changed word will often end with, *-en, -ing,* or *-ed.*	The Rolla won first place in Sun Rayce 99. The Rolla *won* with an average speed of 25.30 mph.	The Rolla, *finishing* with an average speed of 25.30 mph, finished first place in Sun Rayce 99.
		They ship the parts in crates. They *mark* the crates with the words HANDLE WITH CARE.	They ship the parts in crates *marked* with the words HANDLE WITH CARE.
8	Add a group of words that begins with the word *to* to a sentence.	The competitors often left roads, removed fences, and drove across fields. They did this *to avoid* large snowdrifts.	*To avoid* large snowdrifts, the competitors often left roads, removed fences, and drove across fields.

		We blew the tube up and filled it with water. We wanted *to find* the leak.	We blew the tube up and filled it with water *to find* the leak.
9	Add to a sentence a group of words that gives information about a person by using the word *who*.	The third member of the French team was Captain Hans Hansen. He did not know how to drive.	The third member of the French team was Captain Hans Hansen, *who* did not know how to drive.
		The German Protos automobile was built by special order of Kaiser Wilhelm. Kaiser Wilhelm was the German ruler.	The German Protos automobile was built by special order of Kaiser Wilhelm, *who* was the German ruler.
10	Add information to a sentence using the words *which* or *that*.	The huge thirty-seven-inch wheels carried tires. The tires were studded with short steel spikes for driving in snow.	The huge thirty-seven-inch wheels carried tires *that* were studded with short steel spikes for driving in snow.
		The German team skipped a thousand miles of driving. Their trip did not include the distance from Utah to the west coast of the United States.	The German team skipped a thousand miles of driving, *which* included the distance from Utah to the west coast of the United States.
11	Add information to a sentence using the words *when* or where.	The intense heat was almost unbearable. They were driving in Arizona.	The intense heat was almost unbearable *when* they were driving in Arizona.

		The winning Thomas crew arrived in New York City. The waiting crowds went wild.	The winning Thomas crew arrived in New York City, *where* the waiting crowds went wild.
12	Combine two sentences to show *cause and effect* using a transition word.	The officials penalized the German team fifteen days. The German team had taken two shortcuts.	The officials penalized the German team fifteen days *because* the German team had taken two shortcuts.
	Some words that show cause and effect are *so, because, therefore, for, since,* and *consequently.*	The American team reported undrivable conditions in Alaska. The race officials in Paris changed the route of the race.	The American team reported undrivable conditions in Alaska; *therefore*, the race officials in Paris changed the route of the race.
13	Combine two sentences to show *sequence* using a transition word.	The wheels of the cars would not turn in the soft sand. The racers tore strips of cloth to place under the wheels for traction.	*When* the wheels of the cars would not turn in the soft sand, the racers tore strips of cloth to place under the wheels for traction.
	Some words that show sequence are *then, while, when, meanwhile,* and *finally.*	The rear fenders of the 1907 Thomas Flyer were removed. A plank was attached as a shelf to each side of the car.	The rear fenders of the 1907 Thomas Flyer were removed; *then*, a plank was attached as a shelf to each side of the car.
14	Combine two sentences to show that one idea *depends on* another idea.	The American team could drive through Russia. They needed to find gasoline for their car.	The American team could drive through Russia *as long as* they could find gasoline for their car.

Some words that show dependence or condition are *if, as long as,* and *provided that.*

The Thomas team would close the gap with the Protos.
They needed to catch the ferry in time.

The Thomas team would close the gap with the Protos *if* they caught the ferry in time.

15. Combine two sentences to show that two ideas are in contrast with each other.

Some words that show contrast are *although, however, nevertheless, though,* and *on the contrary.*

Most of the people thought the race was sensible.
Some people had strong objections to it.

Most of the people thought the race was sensible *although* some people had strong objections to it.

The Zust snapped two springs, punctured a gas tank, and broke a wheel.
The team was not deterred.

The Zust snapped two springs, punctured a gas tank, and broke a wheel; *nevertheless,* the team was not deterred.

Index

SENTENCE COMBINING CHART

	TECHNIQUE	EXAMPLES	COMBINED
1	Join two sentences using *and, but, or, for, so,* or *yet.*	Baseball player Ty Cobb is known for stealing bases. Hank Aaron holds the record for hitting home runs.	Baseball player Ty Cobb is known for stealing bases, *and* Hank Aaron holds the record for hitting home runs.
2	Join closely related ideas.	Calamity Jane was a Pony Express rider. She boasted about her bravery. She boasted about her marksmanship.	Pony Express rider Calamity Jane boasted about her bravery and her marksmanship.
3	Combine single words from sentences without any changes in word form.	Helen Keller was blind. Helen Keller was deaf. Helen Keller could read. Helen Keller could write. Helen Keller could communicate with sign language.	Blind and deaf, Helen Keller could read, write, and communicate with sign language.
4	Combine single words from sentences with changes in word forms.	Pulitzer Prizes are prestigious awards given for excellence in American journalism, literature, and music. Pulitzer Prizes are annual awards.	Pulitzer Prizes are prestigious awards given *annually* for excellence in American journalism, literature, and music.
5	Combine groups of words from sentences without changes in form.	Prohibition was the outlawing of alcoholic beverages by Constitutional amendment. The period of Prohibition was between 1920 and 1933.	Prohibition, between 1920 and 1933, was the outlawing of alcoholic beverages by Constitutional amendment.
6	Add a group of words to a sentence, separating the group with a comma or pair of commas.	Fiorella LaGuardia read the comics over the radio during a newspaper strike in New York City. Fiorella LaGuardia was a beloved mayor of New York City.	Fiorella LaGuardia, *a beloved mayor of New York City,* read the comics over the radio during a newspaper strike in New York City.
7	Add a group of words to a sentence by changing the form of the first word. The changed word will often end with *-en, -ing,* or *-ed.*	Charles Lindberg was the first aviator to fly nonstop across the Atlantic Ocean. His nickname was the "Lone Eagle."	Charles Lindberg, *nicknamed* the "Lone Eagle, was the first aviator to fly nonstop across the Atlantic Ocean.
8	Add a group of words that begins with the word *to* to a sentence.	Social reformer Carry Nation often swung a hatchet at bars and saloons, doing considerable damage. She was promoting abstinence from alcohol.	*To* promote abstinence from alcohol, social reformer Carry Nation often swung a hatchet at bars and saloons, doing considerable damage.